Ruskin on Art and Artists

RUSKIN ON ART AND ARTISTS

DOVER THRIFT EDITIONS

John Ruskin

Edited by
Bob Blaisdell

DOVER PUBLICATIONS
GARDEN CITY, NEW YORK

DOVER THRIFT EDITIONS

General Editor: Susan L. Rattiner
Editor of This Volume: Gregory Koutrouby

Ruskin on Art and Artists is a new work, first published by Dover Publications in 2025.

ISBN-13: 978-0-486-85533-2
ISBN-10: 0-486-85533-3

Printed in the United States of America
85533301   2025
www.doverpublications.com

Contents

Introduction

RANGING FROM A few sentences to several dozen, these samplings of dramatic, emphatic, amusing, and exhilarating statements by John Ruskin (1819–1900) about art and artists must be among the most fun pieces of art criticism ever produced:

> The one thing you have to learn—the one power truly called that of "painting"—is to lay on any coloured substance, whatever its consistence may be, (from mortar to ether,) at once, of the exact tint you want, in the exact form you want, and in the exact quantity you want. That is painting. Now, you are well aware that to play on the violin well, requires some practice. Painting is playing on a colour-violin, seventy-times-seven stringed, and inventing your tune as you play it! That is the easy, simple, straightforward business you have to learn.[1]

As Victorian England's preeminent art critic, Ruskin's enthusiasms were and still are infectious. He brims over with passionate pleas and vivid illustrations for the reader to see, or perhaps *feel*, what he, Ruskin, could see. Describing the goals of landscape artists (and, it could be said, for his own books), he writes: "The artist not only places the spectator, but talks to him; makes him a sharer in his own strong feelings and quick thoughts; hurries him away in his own enthusiasm; guides him to all that is beautiful; snatches him from all that is base, and leaves him more than delighted,—ennobled and instructed, under the sense of having not only beheld a new scene, but of having held communion with a new mind, and having been

[1] *The Laws of Fesole*, "Of the Twelve Zodiacal Colours" (1877).

endowed for a time with the keen perception and the impetuous emotion of a nobler and more penetrating intelligence."[2]

The first volume of *Modern Painters*, published anonymously when he was twenty-four, had a famous reader, the novelist Charlotte Brontë, whose response has described those of countless others: "Hitherto I have only had instinct to guide me in judging of art; I feel now as if I had been walking blindfold—this book seems to give me eyes. I do wish I had pictures within reach by which to test the new sense. Who can read these glowing descriptions of Turner's works without longing to see them?" Ruskin had done the hardest and best thing that a critic ever does: excite readers to go look for themselves! Brontë added: "I like this author's style much; there is both energy and beauty in it. I like himself, too, because he is such a hearty admirer. He does not give half-measure of praise or veneration. He eulogizes, he reverences with his whole soul."[3] Later, reading *The Stones of Venice*, Brontë added, wonderfully: "His earnestness even amuses me in certain passages; for I cannot help laughing to think how utilitarians will fume and fret over his deep, serious, and (*they* will think) fanatical reverence for art."[4] It's possible that "fanatical," though, is just right.

His heroes are the representational artists of the past, the British landscape painter J. M. W. Turner (1775–1851) as the great *contemporary* exception, and they are predominantly Italian, primarily Venetian, in particular Titian and Tintoretto (whom he invariably calls Tintoret):

> Titian is always absolutely Right. You may imitate him with entire security that you are doing the best thing that can possibly be done for the purpose in hand. Tintoret is always relatively Right—relatively to his own aims and peculiar powers. But you must quite understand Tintoret before you can be sure what his aim was, and why he was then right in doing what would not be right always. If, however, you take the pains thus to understand him, he becomes entirely instructive and exemplary, just as Titian is; and therefore I have placed him among those

[2] *Modern Painters*, Vol. 1, "Of Ideas of Truth in Their Connection with Those of Beauty and Relation" (1843).

[3] W. G. Collingwood. *The Life of John Ruskin*. Boston: Houghton, Mifflin and Company. 1902. 111–12.

[4] W. G. Collingwood. *The Life of John Ruskin*. 128.

who are "always right," and you can only study him rightly with that reverence for him.[5]

The passages in this anthology show that Ruskin's thoughts are as explosive and free-flowing as lava, and consequently he was not concerned about limiting (or was unable to limit) his thoughts to a specified theme: "his mind always impelled his pen to associate one thing with another. The wandering and often unhappy course of Ruskin's life made him, and his books, 'unstable as water.'"[6]

Readers will find some of his finest statements on sculpture in *Modern Painters*; some of his most famous statements on Turner's paintings occur in *The Stones of Venice*; and some of his most compelling autobiographical anecdotes occur not in his autobiography or letters, but in lectures and essays on art, geology, and society. His social and economic writings, particularly *Unto This Last* (1860), later inspired Mahatma Gandhi and Leo Tolstoy. He was a popular and dynamic lecturer, and delivered nearly two hundred, many of which he gave in his fifties and sixties, when he was a professor at Oxford.

Readers might be surprised by his sarcastic remarks about Leonardo da Vinci, Michelangelo, and Rembrandt, who, while he granted them their genius, he believed were *less* great and well-rounded than his favorites. Readers might also be surprised by his repeated snubbings of the Dutch, Flemish, and German painters and by the absence (in this anthology) of any notice of artists from the Middle East, Africa, Asia, or the Americas. Although he did eventually write a little bit about women artists, there is nothing of them mentioned here. He had his specialties, and while his bold, clear-cut statements seem to suggest comprehensiveness, Ruskin's "judgments on painting," writes Tim Hilton, "were scarcely ever tempered by the local and comparative methods of the art historian."[7]

⋆

The only child of Scotch evangelical first cousins, Ruskin grew up in London, sheltered and spoiled, precocious but scarcely socializing with other children. He was unusually devoted to his parents, and they to him; he was regularly living and traveling with them into his forties. Ruskin's well-read father was an astute wine merchant, who

[5] *The Two Paths,* Appendix 1, "Right and Wrong" (1858).
[6] Tim Hilton. *John Ruskin: The Later Years.* 182.
[7] Tim Hilton. *John Ruskin: The Early Years.* 95.

provided his son with the financial means to devote himself to study and writing. His reverent mother raised him on the Bible, which he came to know backward and forward, though eventually he lost his faith in Christianity's truth. A highly skilled draftsman, Ruskin painstakingly drew the subjects of the art, landscape, and architecture that he wrote about, but he felt he never attained the proficiency or freedom that true artists had.

While at Oxford University, where he studied English literature, he wrote the first of his five volumes of *Modern Painters* (1843), in which, besides championing Turner's paintings, was a venue where he made observations on everything from sculpture to geology, botany, religion, himself, and society. Before finishing the loosely connected and loosely organized *Modern Painters* volumes (the last came out in 1860), Ruskin also wrote *The Seven Lamps of Architecture* (1849) and *The Stones of Venice* (three volumes, 1851–1853), which are *mostly* about architecture and sculpture, but also about painting and his other passions.

"Ruskin was a tall slight young fellow whose piercing frank blue eyes lookt through you and drew you to him," recalled one of his friends, F. J. Furnivall, who met him around 1850. "A fair man, with rough light hair and reddish whiskers, in a dark blue frock coat with velvet collar, bright Oxford blue stock, black trousers and velvet slippers—how vivid he is to me still . . . ! I never met any man whose charm of manner at all approach Ruskin's. Partly feminine it was, no doubt; but the delicacy, the sympathy, the gentleness and affectionateness of his way, the fresh and penetrating things he said, the boyish fun, the earnestness, the interest he showed in all deep matters, combined to make a whole which I have never seen equaled."[8]

While the 1840s–1860s were the most productive and influential period of his renown as an art and architecture critic, during this time his marriage (1848–1854) to Euphemia Gray was almost a matter of indifference to him; the relationship remained unconsummated. (She was granted an annulment, and married John Everett Millais, a Pre-Raphaelite painter whose friendship Ruskin had cultivated and whose work Ruskin had praised.) For the most part, Ruskin shrugged off the gossip. As he admitted to a friend, the failure of his domestic life had been of less import to him than the fact that Turner had died, in 1851, and that his beloved Venice's thirteenth-century architecture was being destroyed by "restoration."

[8] Tim Hilton. *John Ruskin: The Early Years*. 151.

Ruskin had the Victorian virtues of industriousness, philanthropy, and scientific curiosity, but he also embodied and expressed some of the era's and empire's vices: religious and racial bigotry, male chauvinism, warmongering patriotism, and hysterical prudery coupled with a disabling attraction for adolescent girls. Ruskin had a dynamic personality with dramatic imbalances in his character. Even as a young man he seemed to deliberately work himself to physical and mental exhaustion. For relaxation he practiced gardening, road making, bricklaying, and mineralogy. For years he gave drawing lessons by mail to young or working people. These letters evolved into the giddy *The Elements of Drawing* (1857).

The year his marriage ended, Ruskin began teaching at London's Working Men's College. His goal, he discovered, was for his students to learn enough so that they could simply take *pleasure* in making pictures and thereby also appreciate art history's masterpieces. In the 1860s, he began writing more about social and economic issues and less about painting and architecture. The most consuming and disturbing passion of the 1860s and early 1870s, however, concerned a young Irish woman whom he had tutored in drawing while she was still a girl, Rose La Touche. He suffered over and worshipped her; he repeatedly proposed, but sensibly she would not marry him. When La Touche died at the age of twenty-seven in 1875, he began seeing her image in various artworks (particularly Vittore Carpaccio's painting *The Dream of St. Ursula*), and believed in her ghostly visitations. He fell prey to manic-depressive breakdowns more often and with more incapacitating results in the 1870s and 1880s. He was overcome by a spell of insanity in 1889, from which he never recovered.

★

Everything Ruskin published in his lifetime is available in the public domain. The standard edition, *The Works of John Ruskin* (thirty-nine volumes, 1903–1912), edited by E. T. Cook and Alexander Wedderburn, who supply detailed background and scholarship, has been and is being supplemented by publications of his diaries and letters.[9] There is no single exemplary title of Ruskin's, but the most consistently entertaining are, in this editor's opinion, *The Seven Lamps of Architecture* and *The Elements of Drawing*; the grandest and probably

[9] For steering me toward passages I overlooked, I am indebted to Cook and Wedderburn, the previous anthology editors and Ruskin's biographers. See the Selected Bibliography, page 119.

most important are the multivolume *Modern Painters* and *The Stones of Venice*. Among the several collections of his lectures, *The Two Paths* is particularly wonderful, and the format makes it possible to imagine him in a happy declamatory mode.[10] In one lecture at Oxford in 1870, he declared (perhaps shouted, as he renders it in all-caps in the book): "THE HIGHEST THING THAT ART CAN DO IS TO SET BEFORE YOU THE TRUE IMAGE OF THE PRESENCE OF A NOBLE HUMAN BEING. IT HAS NEVER DONE MORE THAN THIS, AND IT OUGHT NOT TO DO LESS."[11]

His *Fors Clavigera* (1871–1884), a series of occasional public letters on random social and yet sometimes very personal topics (including a fascinating account of one of his falls into and recovery from madness), was the major project of the end of his working life, in which he could address—he gleefully told his by-subscription readers—*anything in the world*. The patchy autobiography *Praeterita* (1885–89), completed between his bouts with mental illness, takes a deliberately different tone from his other writing. It is wistful and light (he completely avoids disquieting topics, including his marriage), but is also a sad relaxation of his enthusiasm, insight, and wit.

For a comprehensive appreciation of his character and thought, see Tim Hilton's *John Ruskin: The Early Years* (1985) and *John Ruskin: The Later Years* (2000).

*

As I weighed and sifted through the quotations, eight themes suggested themselves. Due to Ruskin's mercurial attention, they are necessarily loose and nonrestrictive topics. He is, all to the good, hard to pin down. Ruskin's father pointed out to his son that "your books will resemble a conjuror's box which you open expecting one thing and find another."[12] Curious readers will find gems of Ruskinian brilliance in unlikely places. His focus on one particular artist usually put him in mind of others, as will be obvious in the opening section, "Artists in Comparison and Contrast." The only artist in his own category is J. M. W. Turner. For page references to particular artists,

[10] For a treat, listen to *The Two Paths* as read on Librivox, particularly the sections read by Todd Ulbrich.

[11] *Lectures on Art, Delivered Before the University of Oxford in Hilary Term, 1870* ("The Relation of Art to Religion").

[12] John Dixon Hunt. *The Wider Sea: A Life of John Ruskin*. London: Dent. 1982. 206.

see the Index of Artists, which provides their full or common names and their birth and death dates.

In each thematic section, I arrange the quotations chronologically, by the year of the work's first publication, though time does not seem to neatly frame Ruskin either. Note that the lectures, though sometimes given in a previous year, took their final form in the book publication (that is, they were not transcripts, as Ruskin improvised from his own prepared notes). I have retained the spelling and punctuation that Ruskin used in the various contemporary editions of his work.

—Bob Blaisdell
March 2025

Artists in Comparison and Contrast

{"Ghirlandajo and Titian painted men, but could not angels; Duccio and Angelico painted Saints, but could not senators"}

THE FACT IS, that all artists are primarily divided into the two great groups of Imitators and Suggesters—their falling into one or other being dependent partly on disposition, and partly on the matter they have to subdue—(thus Perugino imitates line by line with penciled gold, the hair which Nino Pisano can only suggest by a gilded marble mass, both having the will of representation alike). [. . .] artists proper, are appointed, each with his peculiar gift and affection, over the several orders and classes of things natural, to be by them illumined and set forth.

And that is God's doing and distributing; and none is rashly to be thought inferior to another, as if by his own fault; nor any of them stimulated to emulation, and changing places with others, although their allotted tasks be of different dignities, and their granted instruments of different keenness; for in none of them can there be a perfection or balance of all human attributes;—the great colourist becomes gradually insensible to the refinements of form which he at first intentionally omitted; the master of line is inevitably dead to many of the delights of colour; the study of the true or ideal human form is inconsistent with the love of its most spiritual expressions. To one it is intrusted to record the historical realities of his age; in him the perception of character is subtle, and that of abstract beauty in measure diminished; to another, removed to the desert, or inclosed in the cloister, is given, not the noting of things transient, but the revealing of things eternal. Ghirlandajo and Titian painted men, but could not angels; Duccio and Angelico painted Saints, but could not senators. One is ordered to copy material form lovingly and slowly—his the fine finger and patient will: to another are sent visions and dreams upon the bed—his the hand fearful and swift, and impulse of passion irregular and wild.

—Review of *The History of Christian Art, Quarterly Review* (1847)

★

{"The mind which molds and summons cannot at will transmute itself into that which clings and contemplates"}

If human life were endless, or human spirit could fit its compass to its will, it is possible a perfection might be reached which should unite the majesty of invention with the meekness of love. We might conceive that the thought, arrested by the readiest means, and at first represented by the boldest symbols, might afterwards be set forth with solemn and studied expression, and that the power might know no weariness in clothing which had known no restraint in creating. But dilation and contraction are for molluscs, not for men; we are not ringed into flexibility like worms, nor gifted with opposite sight and mutable colour like chameleons. The mind which molds and summons cannot at will transmute itself into that which clings and contemplates; nor is it given to us at once to have the potter's power over the lump, the fire's upon the clay, and the gilder's upon the porcelain. Even the temper in which we behold these various displays of mind must be different; and it admits of more than doubt whether, if the bold work of rapid thought were afterwards in all its forms completed with microscopic care, the result would be other than painful. In the shadow at the foot of Tintoret's picture of the Temptation, lies a broken rock-boulder. The dark ground has been first laid in, of colour nearly uniform; and over it a few, not more than fifteen or twenty, strokes of the brush, loaded with a light gray, have quarried the solid block of stone out of the vacancy. Probably ten minutes are the utmost time which those strokes have occupied, though the rock is some four feet square. It may safely be affirmed that no other method, however laborious, could have reached the truth of form which results from the very freedom with which the conception has been expressed; but it is a truth of the simplest kind—the definition of a stone, rather than the painting of one—and the lights are in some degree dead and cold—the natural consequence of striking a mixed opaque pigment over a dark ground. It would now be possible to treat this skeleton of a stone, which could only have been knit together by Tintoret's rough temper, with the care of a Fleming; to leave its fiercely-stricken lights emanating from a golden ground, to gradate with the pen its ponderous shadows, and in its completion, to dwell with endless and intricate precision upon fibers of moss, bells of heath, blades of grass, and films of lichen. Love like Van Eyck's would separate the fibers as if they were stems of forest, twine the ribbed grass into fanciful articulation, shadow forth capes and islands in the variegated film, and hang the purple bells in counted chiming. A year might pass away, and the work yet be incomplete; yet would the purpose of the great picture have been better answered when all had been achieved? or if so, is it to be wished that a year of the life of Tintoret (could such a thing be conceived possible) had been so devoted?

—"Eastlake on the History of Painting" (1848)

*

{"the business of the painter is to *paint*"}

We ought to be able to tell good painting by a side glance as we pass along a gallery; and, until we can do so, we are not fit to pronounce judgment at all: not that I class this easily visible excellence of painting with the great expressional qualities which time and watchfulness only unfold. I have again and again insisted on the supremacy of these last and shall always continue to do so. But I perceive a tendency among some of the more thoughtful critics of the day to forget that the business of the painter is to *paint*, and so altogether to despise those men, Veronese and Rubens for instance, who were painters, par excellence, and in whom the expressional qualities are subordinate. Now it is well, when we have strong moral or poetical feeling manifested in painting, to mark this as the best part of the work; but it is not well to consider as a thing of small account, the painter's language in which that feeling is conveyed; for if that language be not good and lovely, the man may indeed be a just moralist or a great poet, but he is not a *painter*, and it was wrong of him to paint. He had much better put his morality into sermons, and his poetry into verse, than into a language of which he was not master. And this mastery of the language is that of which we should be cognizant by a glance of the eye; and if that be not found, it is wasted time to look farther: the man has mistaken his vocation, and his expression of himself will be cramped by his awkward efforts to do what he was not fit to do. On the other hand, if the man be a painter indeed, and have the gift of colours and lines, what is in him will come from his hand freely and faithfully; and the language itself is so difficult and so vast, that the mere possession of it argues the man is great, and that his works are worth reading. So that I have never yet seen the case in which this true artistical excellence, visible by the eye-glance, was not the index of some true expressional worth in the work. Neither have I ever seen a good expressional work without high artistical merit [. . .].

—*The Stones of Venice*, Vol. I, "Appendix: Instinctive Judgments" (1851)

★

{Bartolomé Esteban Murillo "might have shown hunger in other ways"}

I doubt not that the reader was surprised when I named Murillo among the men of this third rank. Yet, go into the Dulwich Gallery, and meditate for a little over that much celebrated picture of the two beggar boys, one eating lying on the ground, the other standing beside him. We have among our own painters one who cannot indeed be set beside Murillo as a painter of Madonnas, for he is a pure Naturalist, and, never having seen a Madonna, does not paint any; but who, as a painter of beggar or peasant boys, may be set beside Murillo, or any one else,—W. Hunt.[13] He loves peasant boys, because he finds them more roughly and picturesquely dressed, and more healthily coloured, than others. And he paints all that he sees in them fearlessly; all the health and humor, and freshness, and vitality, together with such awkwardness and stupidity, and what else of negative or positive harm there may be in the creature; but yet so that on the whole we love it, and find it perhaps even beautiful, or if not, at least we see that there is capability of good in it, rather than of evil; and all is lighted up by a sunshine and sweet colour that makes the smock-frock as precious as cloth of gold. But look at those two ragged and vicious vagrants that Murillo has gathered out of the street. You smile at first, because they are eating so naturally, and their roguery is so complete. But is there anything else than roguery there, or was it well for the painter to give his

[13] William Holman Hunt.

time to the painting of those repulsive and wicked children? Do you feel moved with any charity towards children as you look at them? Are we the least more likely to take any interest in ragged schools, or to help the next pauper child that comes in our way, because the painter has shown us a cunning beggar feeding greedily? Mark the choice of the act. He might have shown hunger in other ways, and given interest to even this act of eating, by making the face wasted, or the eye wistful. But he did not care to do this. He delighted merely in the disgusting manner of eating, the food filling the cheek; the boy is not hungry, else he would not turn round to talk and grin as he eats.

But observe another point in the lower figure. It lies so that the sole of the foot is turned towards the spectator; not because it would have lain less easily in another attitude, but that the painter may draw, and exhibit, the grey dust engrained in the foot. Do not call this the painting of nature: it is mere delight in foulness. The lesson, if there be any, in the picture, is not one whit the stronger. We all know that a beggar's bare foot cannot be clean; there is no need to thrust its degradation into the light, as if no human imagination were vigorous enough for its conception.[14]

—*The Stones of Venice*, Vol. II, "The Nature of Gothic" (1853)

★

{"Giotto was to his contemporaries [. . .] a daring naturalist, in defiance of tradition, idealism, and formalism"}

Close imitation of nature. In this one principle lay Giotto's great strength, and the entire secret of the revolution he effected. It was not by greater learning, not by the discovery of new theories of art, not by greater taste, nor by "ideal" principles of selection, that he became the head of the progressive schools of Italy. It was simply by being interested in what was going on around him, by substituting the gestures of living men for conventional attitudes, and portraits of living men for conventional faces, and incidents of every-day life for conventional circumstances, that he became great, and the master of the great. Giotto was to his contemporaries precisely what Millais is to *his* contemporaries,—a daring naturalist, in defiance of tradition, idealism, and formalism. The Giottoesque movement in the

[14] Bartolomé Esteban Murillo, *Boys Eating Grapes and Melon*, c. 1645–46, painting.

fourteenth, and Pre-Raphaelite movement in the nineteenth centuries, are precisely similar in bearing and meaning: both being the protests of vitality against mortality, of spirit against letter, and of truth against tradition: and both, which is the more singular, literally links in one unbroken chain of feeling; for exactly as Niccola Pisano and Giotto were helped by the classical sculptures discovered in their time, the Pre-Raphaelites have been helped by the works of Niccola and Giotto at Pisa and Florence: and thus the fiery cross of truth has been delivered from spirit to spirit, over the dust of intervening generations.

But what, it may be said by the reader, is the use of the works of Giotto to *us*? They may indeed have been wonderful for their time, and of infinite use in that time; but since, after Giotto, came Leonardo and Correggio, what is the use of going back to the ruder art, and republishing it in the year 1854? Why should we fret ourselves to dig down to the root of the tree, when we may at once enjoy its fruit and foliage? I answer, first, that in all matters relating to human intellect, it is a great thing to have hold of the root: that at least we ought to see it, and taste it, and handle it; for it often happens that the root is wholesome when the leaves, however fair, are useless or poisonous. In nine cases out of ten, the first expression of an idea is the most valuable: the idea may afterward be polished and softened, and made more attractive to the general eye; but the first expression of it has a freshness and brightness, like the flash of a native crystal compared to the lustre of glass that has been melted and cut. And in the second place, we ought to measure the value of art less by its executive than by its moral power. Giotto was not indeed one of the most accomplished painters, but he was one of the greatest men who ever lived. He was the first master of his time, in architecture as well as in painting; he was the friend of Dante, and the undisputed interpreter of religious truth, by means of painting, over the whole of Italy. The works of such a man may not be the best to set before children in order to teach them drawing; but they assuredly should be studied with the greatest care by all who are interested in the history of the human mind.

—*Giotto and His Works in Padua* (1854)

⋆

{"let me see with your eyes, and hear with your ears"}

[. . .] the difference between a noble and ignoble painter is in nothing more sharply defined than in this,—that the first wishes to put into his work as much truth as possible, and yet to keep it looking un-real; the second wishes to get through his work lazily, with as little truth as possible, and yet to make it look real; and, so far as they add colour to their abstract sketch, the first realizes for the sake of the colour, and the second colours for the sake of the realization.

And then, lastly, it is another infinite advantage possessed by the picture, that in these various differences from reality it becomes the expression of the power and intelligence of a companionable human soul. In all this choice, arrangement, penetrative sight, and kindly guidance, we recognize a supernatural operation, and perceive, not merely the landscape or incident as in a mirror, but, besides, the presence of what, after all, may perhaps be the most wonderful piece of divine work in the whole matter—the great human spirit through which it is manifested to us. So that, although with respect to many important scenes, it might, as we saw above, be one of the most precious gifts that could be given us to see them with *our own eyes*, yet also in many things it is more desirable to be permitted to see them with the eyes of others; and although, to the small, conceited, and affected painter displaying his narrow knowledge and tiny dexterities, our only word may be, "Stand aside from between that nature and me," yet to the great imaginative painter—greater a million times in every faculty of soul than we—our word may wisely be, "Come between this nature and me—this nature which is too great and too wonderful for me; temper it for me, interpret it to me; let me see with your eyes, and hear with your ears, and have help and strength from your great spirit."

—*Modern Painters*, Vol. III, "Of the Use of Pictures" (1856)

★

{"when Titian or Tintoret look at a human being, they see at a glance the whole of its nature"}

[. . .] not only is there but one way of *doing* things rightly, but there is only one way of *seeing* them, and that is, seeing the whole of them, without any choice, or more intense perception of one point than another, owing to our special idiosyncrasies. Thus, when Titian or

Tintoret look at a human being, they see at a glance the whole of its nature, outside and in; all that it has of form, of colour, of passion, or of thought; saintliness, and loveliness; fleshly body, and spiritual power; grace, or strength, or softness, or whatsoever other quality, those men will see to the full, and so paint, that, when narrower people come to look at what they have done, every one may, if he chooses, find his own special pleasure in the work. The sensualist will find sensuality in Titian; the thinker will find thought; the saint, sanctity; the colourist, colour; the anatomist, form; and yet the picture will never be a popular one in the full sense, for none of these narrower people will find their special taste so alone consulted, as that the qualities which would ensure their gratification shall be sifted or separated from others; they are checked by the presence of the other qualities which ensure the gratification of other men. Thus, Titian is not soft enough for the sensualist, Correggio suits him better; Titian is not defined enough for the formalist,—Leonardo suits him better; Titian is not pure enough for the religionist,—Raphael suits him better; Titian is not polite enough for the man of the world,—Van Dyck suits him better; Titian is not forcible enough for the lovers of the picturesque,—Rembrandt suits him better. So Correggio is popular with a certain set, and Van Dyck with a certain set, and Rembrandt with a certain set. All are great men, but of inferior stamp, and therefore Van Dyck is popular, and Rembrandt is popular,[15] but nobody cares much at heart about Titian; only there is a strange under-current of everlasting murmur about his name, which means the deep consent of all great men that he is greater than they—the consent of those who, having sat long enough at his feet, have found in that restrained harmony of his strength there are indeed depths of each balanced power more wonderful than all those separate manifestations in inferior painters: that there is a softness more exquisite than Correggio's, a purity loftier than Leonardo's, a force mightier than Rembrandt's, a sanctity more solemn even than Raffaelle's.[16]

Do not suppose that in saying this of Titian, I am returning to the old eclectic theories of Bologna; for all those eclectic theories, observe, were based, not upon an endeavour to unite the various characters of nature (which it is possible to do), but the various narrownesses of taste, which it is impossible to do. Rubens is not more

[15] {Ruskin's note.} And Murillo, of all true painters the narrowest, feeblest, and most superficial, for those reasons the most popular.

[16] Titian, *Flora*, 1516–20, painting.

vigorous than Titian, but less vigorous; but because he is so narrow-minded as to enjoy vigour only, he refuses to give the other qualities of nature, which would interfere with that vigour and with our perception of it. Again, Rembrandt is not a greater master of chiaroscuro than Titian;—he is a less master, but because he is so narrow-minded as to enjoy chiaroscuro only, he withdraws from you the splendour of hue which would interfere with this, and gives you only the shadow in which you can at once feel it.

Now all these specialties have their own charm in their own way: and there are times when the particular humour of each man is refreshing to us from its very distinctness; but the effort to add any other qualities to this refreshing one instantly takes away the distinctiveness, and therefore the exact character to be enjoyed in its appeal to a particular humour in us. Our enjoyment arose from a weakness meeting a weakness, from a partiality in the painter fitting to a partiality in us, and giving us sugar when we wanted sugar, and myrrh when we wanted myrrh; but sugar and myrrh are not meat: and when we want meat and bread, we must go to better men.

—*The Two Paths*, "The Unity of Art" (1858)

*

{"Now the question is, whether, as students, we are to study only these mightiest men"}

[. . .] in Turner's lifetime, when people first looked at him, those who liked rainy weather, said he was not equal to Copley Fielding; but those who looked at Turner long enough found that he could be much more wet than Copley Fielding, when he chose. The people who liked force, said that "Turner was not strong enough for them; he was effeminate; they liked De Wint,—nice strong tone;—or Cox—great, greeny, dark masses of colour—solemn feeling of the freshness and depth of nature;—they liked Cox—Turner was too hot for them." Had they looked long enough they would have found that he had far more force than De Wint, far more freshness than Cox when he chose,—only united with other elements; and that he didn't choose to be cool, if nature had appointed the weather to be hot. The people who liked Prout said "Turner had not firmness of hand—he did not know enough about architecture—he was not picturesque enough." Had they looked at his architecture long, they would have found that it contained subtle picturesquenesses, infinitely more picturesque than anything of Prout's. People who liked Callcott said that "Turner was not correct or pure enough—had no classical taste." Had they looked at Turner long enough they would have found him as severe, when he chose, as the greater Poussin;—Callcott, a mere vulgar imitator of other men's high breeding. And so throughout with all thoroughly great men, their strength is not seen at first, precisely because they unite, in due place and measure, every great quality.

—*The Two Paths*, "The Unity of Art" (1858)

★

{Of Joshua Reynolds, "the prince of portrait painters," and of Velázquez, "among the very greatest of painters"}

I am inclined to think that, considering all the disadvantages of circumstances and education under which his genius was developed, there was perhaps hardly ever born a man with a more intense and innate gift of insight into nature than our own Sir Joshua Reynolds. Considered as a painter of individuality in the human form and mind, I think him, even as it is, the prince of portrait painters. Titian paints nobler pictures, and Van Dyck had nobler subjects, but neither of them entered so subtly as Sir Joshua did into the minor varieties of human heart and temper; arid when you consider that, with a frightful conventionality of social habitude all around him, he yet conceived the simplest types of all feminine and childish loveliness;—that in a northern climate, and with gray, and white, and black, as the principal colours around him, he yet became a colourist who can be crushed by none, even of the Venetians;—and that with Dutch painting and Dresden china for the prevailing types of art in the saloons of his day, he threw himself at once at the feet of the great masters of Italy, and arose from their feet to share their throne—I know not that in the whole history of art you can produce another instance of so strong, so unaided, so unerring an instinct for all that was true, pure, and noble. Now, do you recollect the evidence respecting the character of this man,—the two points of bright peculiar evidence given by the sayings of the two greatest literary men of his day, Johnson and Goldsmith? Johnson, who, as you know, was always Reynolds' attached friend, had but one complaint to make against him, that he hated nobody:—"Reynolds," he said, "you hate no one living; I like a good hater!" [. . .]

The other painter whom I would give you as an instance of this gentleness is a man of another nation, on the whole I suppose one of the most cruel civilized nations in the world—the Spaniards. They produced but one great painter, only one; but he among the very greatest of painters, Velásquez.[17] You would not suppose, from looking at Velásquez' portraits generally, that he was an especially kind or good man; you perceive a peculiar sternness about them; for they were as true as steel, and the persons whom he had to paint being not generally kind or good people, they were stern in expression, and Velásquez gave the sternness; but he had precisely the same intense perception of truth, the same marvellous instinct for the rendering of all natural soul and all natural form that our Reynolds had.

—*The Two Paths*, "The Unity of Art" (1858)

★

{"You may be led wrong by Tintoret in many respects, wrong by Raphael in more; all that you learn from Titian will be right"}

Titian is much the safest master for you. [. . .] Titian's power is simply the power of doing right. Whatever came before Titian, he did wholly as it *ought* to be done. Do not suppose that now in recommending Titian to you so strongly, and speaking of nobody else to-night, I am retreating in anywise from what some of you may perhaps recollect in my works, the enthusiasm with which I have always spoken of another Venetian painter. There are three Venetians who are never separated in my mind—Titian, Veronese, and Tintoret. They all have their own unequalled gifts, and Tintoret especially has imagination and depth of soul which I think renders him indisputably the greatest man; but, equally indisputably, Titian is the greatest painter; and therefore the greatest painter who ever lived. You may be led wrong by Tintoret in many respects, wrong by Raphael in more; all that you learn from Titian will be right. Then, with Titian, take Leonardo, Rembrandt, and Albert Dürer. I name those three masters for this reason: Leonardo has powers of subtle drawing which are peculiarly applicable in many ways to the drawing of fine ornament, and are very useful for all students. Rembrandt and Dürer are the only men whose actual work of hand you can have to look at; you can have Rembrandt's etchings, or

[17] Diego Velázquez, *Portrait of Pope Innocent X*, 1650, painting.

Dürer's engravings actually hung in your schools; and it is a main point for the student to see the real thing, and avoid judging of masters at second-hand.

—*The Two Paths*, "The Unity of Art" (1858)

★

{"all blame which I express in this sweeping way is trustworthy"}

Artists are divided by an impassable gulf into the men who can paint, and who cannot. The men who can paint often fall short of what they should have done;—are repressed, or defeated, or otherwise rendered inferior one to another: still there is an everlasting barrier between them and the men who cannot paint—who can only in various popular ways pretend to paint. And if once you know the difference, there is always some good to be got by looking at a real painter—seldom anything but mischief to be got out of a false one; but do not suppose real painters are common. I do not speak of living men; but among those who labour no more, in this England of ours, since it first had a school, we have had only five real painters;—Reynolds, Gainsborough, Hogarth, Richard Wilson, and Turner.

The reader may, perhaps, think I have forgotten Wilkie. No. I once much overrated him as an expressional draughtsman, not having then studied the figure long enough to be able to detect superficial sentiment. But his colour I have never praised; it is entirely false and valueless. And it would be unjust to English art if I did not here express my regret that the admiration of Constable, already harmful enough in England, is extending even into France. There was, perhaps, the making, in Constable, of a second or third-rate painter, if any careful discipline had developed in him the instincts which, though unparalleled for narrowness, were, as far as they went, true. But as it is, he is nothing more than an industrious and innocent amateur blundering his way to a superficial expression of one or two popular aspects of common nature.

And my readers may depend upon it, that all blame which I express in this sweeping way is trustworthy. I have often had to repent of overpraise of inferior men; and continually to repent of insufficient praise of great men; but of broad condemnation, never. For I do not speak it but after the most searching examination of the matter, and under stern sense of need for it: so that whenever the reader is entirely shocked by what I say, he may be assured every word is true.[18] It is just because it so much offends him, that it was necessary: and knowing that it must offend him, I should not have ventured to say it, without certainty of its truth. I say "certainty," for it is just as possible to be certain whether the drawing of a tree or a stone is true or false, as whether the drawing of a triangle is; and what I mean primarily by saying that a picture is in all respects worthless, is that it is in all respects False: which is not a matter of opinion at all, but a matter of ascertainable fact, such as I never assert till I have ascertained.

—*The Two Paths*, Appendix 1, "Right and Wrong" (1858)

★

{"You may imitate {Titian} with entire security that you are doing the best thing that can possibly be done for the purpose in hand"}

Titian is always absolutely Right. You may imitate him with entire security that you are doing the best thing that can possibly be done for the purpose in hand. Tintoret is always relatively Right—relatively to his own aims and peculiar powers. But you must quite understand Tintoret before you can be sure what his aim was, and why he was then right in doing what would not be right always. If, however, you take the pains thus to understand him, he becomes entirely instructive and exemplary, just as Titian is; and therefore I have placed him among those who are "always right," and you can only study him rightly with that reverence for him.

Then the artists who are named as "admitting question of right and wrong," are those who from some mischance of circumstance or shortcoming in their education, do not always do right, even with relation to their own aims and powers.

Take for example the quality of imperfection in drawing form. There are many pictures of Tintoret in which the trees are drawn with a few curved flourishes of the brush instead of leaves. That is (absolutely) wrong. If you copied the tree as a model, you would be going very wrong indeed. But it is relatively, and for Tintoret's purposes, right. In the nature of the superficial work you will find

[18] [*Ruskin's footnote.*] He must, however, be careful to distinguish blame—however strongly expressed, of some special fault or error in a true painter,—from these general statements of inferiority or worthlessness. Thus he will find me continually laughing at Wilson's tree-painting; not because Wilson could not paint, but because he had never looked at a tree.

there must have been a cause for it. Somebody perhaps wanted the picture in a hurry to fill a dark corner. Tintoret good-naturedly did all he could—painted the figures tolerably—had five minutes left only for the trees, when the servant came. "Let him wait another five minutes." And this is the best foliage we can do in the time. Entirely, admirably, unsurpassably right, under the conditions. Titian would not have worked under them, but Tintoret was kinder and humbler; yet he may lead you wrong if you don't understand him. Or, perhaps, another day, somebody came in while Tintoret was at work, who tormented Tintoret. An ignoble person! Titian would have been polite to him, and gone on steadily with his trees. Tintoret cannot stand the ignobleness; it is unendurably repulsive and discomfiting to him. "The Black Plague take him—and the trees, too! Shall such a fellow see me paint!" And the trees go all to pieces. This, in you, would be mere ill-breeding and ill-temper. In Tintoret it was one of the necessary conditions of his intense sensibility; had he been capable, then, of keeping his temper, he could never have done his greatest works. Let the trees go to pieces, by all means; it is quite right they should; he is always right.

But in a background of Gainsborough you would find the trees unjustifiably gone to pieces. The carelessness of form there is definitely purposed by him;—adopted as an advisable thing; and therefore it is both absolutely and relatively wrong;—it indicates his being imperfectly educated as a painter, and not having brought out all his powers. It may still happen that the man whose work thus partially erroneous is greater far, than others who have fewer faults. Gainsborough's and Reynolds' wrongs are more charming than almost anybody else's right. Still, they occasionally *are* wrong—but the Venetians and Velásquez, never.

—*The Two Paths*, Appendix 1, "Right and Wrong" (1858)

★

{"the best Dutch painters do not care about the people, but about the lustres on them"}

You will find that the best Dutch painters do not care about the people, but about the lustres on them. Paulus Potter, their best herd and cattle painter, does not care even for sheep, but only for wool; regards not cows, but cowhide. He attains great dexterity in drawing tufts and locks, lingers in the little parallel ravines and furrows of fleece that open across sheep's backs as they turn; is unsurpassed in twisting a horn or pointing a nose; but he cannot paint eyes, nor perceive any condition of an animal's mind, except its desire of grazing. Cuyp can, indeed, paint sunlight, the best that Holland's sun can show; he is a man of large natural gift, and sees broadly, nay, even seriously; finds out—a wonderful thing for men to find out in those days—that there are reflections in water, and that boats require often to be painted upside down. A brewer by trade, he feels the quiet of a summer afternoon, and his work will make you marvelously drowsy. It is good for nothing else that I know of: strong; but unhelpful and unthoughtful. Nothing happens in his pictures, except some indifferent persons asking the way of somebody else, who, by their cast of countenance, seems not likely to know it. For farther entertainment perhaps a red cow and a white one; or puppies at play, not playfully; the man's heart not going even with the puppies. Essentially he sees nothing but the shine on the flaps of their ears.

Observe always, the fault lies not in the things being little, or the incident being slight. Titian could have put issues of life and death into the face of a man asking the way; nay, into the back of him, had he so chosen. He has put a whole scheme of dogmatic theology into a row of bishops' backs at the Louvre. And for dogs, Velásquez has made some of them nearly as grand as his surly kings.

—*Modern Painters*, Vol. V, "Rubens and Cuyp" (1860)

★

{"Why it is, that in Sir Joshua's girl, [. . .] we always think first of the Ladyhood; but in Giotto's, of the Womanhood?"}

Why did not Sir Joshua—or could not—or would not Sir Joshua—paint Madonnas? neither he, nor his great rival-friend Gainsborough? Both of them painters of women, such as since Giorgione and Correggio had not been; both painters of men, such as had not been since Titian. How is it that these English friends can so brightly paint that particular order of humanity which we call "gentlemen and ladies," but neither heroes, nor saints, nor angels? Can it be because they were both country-bred boys, and for ever after strangely sensitive to courtliness? Why, Giotto also was a country-bred boy. Allegri's native Correggio, Titian's Cadore, were but hill villages; yet these men painted, not the court, nor the drawing-room, but the Earth: and not a little of Heaven besides: while our good Sir Joshua never trusts himself outside the park palings. He could not even have drawn the strawberry girl, unless she had got through a gap in them—or rather, I think, she must have been let in at the porter's lodge, for her strawberries are in a pottle, ready for the ladies at the Hall. Giorgione would have set them, wild and fragrant, among their leaves, in her hand. Between his fairness, and Sir Joshua's May-fairness, there is a strange, impassable limit—as of the white reef that in Pacific isles encircles their inner lakelets, and shuts them from the surf and sound of sea. Clear and calm they rest, reflecting fringed shadows of the palm-trees, and the passing of fretted clouds across their own sweet circle of blue sky. But beyond, and round and round their coral bar, lies the blue of sea and heaven together—blue of eternal deep.

You will find it a pregnant question, if you follow it forth, and leading to many others, not trivial, Why it is, that in Sir Joshua's girl, or Gainsborough's, we always think first of the Ladyhood; but in Giotto's, of the Womanhood? Why, in Sir Joshua's hero, or Van Dyck's, it is always the Prince or the Sir whom we see first; but in Titian's, the man.

Not that Titian's gentlemen are less finished than Sir Joshua's; but their gentlemanliness is not the principal thing about them; their manhood absorbs, conquers, wears it as a despised thing. Nor—and this is another stern ground of separation—will Titian make a gentleman of everyone he paints. He will make him so if he is so, not otherwise; and this not merely in general servitude to truth, but because in his sympathy with deeper humanity, the courtier is not more interesting to him than anyone else. "You have learned to dance and fence; you can speak with clearness, and think with precision; your hands are small, your senses acute, and your features well-shaped. Yes: I see all this in you, and will do it justice. You shall stand as none but a well-bred man could stand; and your fingers shall fall on the sword-hilt as no fingers could but those that knew the grasp of it. But for the rest, this grisly fisherman, with rusty cheek and rope-frayed hand, is a man as well as you, and might possibly make several of you, if souls were divisible. His bronze colour is quite as interesting to me, Titian, as your paleness, and his hoary spray of stormy hair takes the light as well as your waving curls. Him also I will paint, with such picturesqueness as he may have; yet not putting the picturesqueness first in him, as in you I have not put the gentlemanliness first. In him I see a strong human creature, contending with all hardship: in you also a human creature, uncontending, and possibly not strong. Contention or strength, weakness or picturesqueness, and all other such accidents in either, shall have due place. But the immortality and miracle of you—this clay that burns, this colour that changes—are in truth the awful things in both: these shall be first painted—and last."

With which question respecting treatment of character we have to connect also this further one: How is it that the attempts of so great painters as Reynolds and Gainsborough are, beyond portraiture, limited almost like children's? No domestic drama—no history—no noble natural scenes, far less any religious subject:—only market carts; girls with pigs; woodmen going home to supper; watering-places; gray cart-horses in fields, and such like. [. . .]

In some degree it may indeed be true that the modesty and sense of the English painters are the causes of their simple practice. All that they did, they did well, and attempted nothing over which conquest was doubtful. They knew they could paint men and women: it did not follow that they could paint angels. Their own gifts never appeared to them so great as to call for serious question as to the use to be made of them. "They could mix colours and catch likeness—yes; but were they therefore able to teach religion, or reform the world? To support themselves honorably, pass the hours of life happily, please their friends, and leave no enemies, was not this all that duty could require, or prudence recommend? Their own art was, it seemed, difficult enough to employ all their genius: was it reasonable to hope also to be poets or theologians? Such men had, indeed, existed; but the age of miracles and prophets was long past; nor, because they could seize the trick of an expression, or the turn of a head, had they any right to think themselves able to conceive heroes with Homer, or gods with Michael Angelo."

Such was, in the main, their feeling: wise, modest, unenvious, and unambitious. Meaner men, their contemporaries or successors, raved of high art with incoherent passion; arrogated to themselves an equality with the masters of elder time, and declaimed against the degenerate tastes of a public which acknowledged not the return of the Heraclidæ. But the two great—the two only painters of their age—happy in a reputation founded as deeply in the heart as in the judgment of mankind, demanded no higher function than that of soothing the domestic affections; and achieved for themselves at last an immortality not the less noble, because in their lifetime they had concerned themselves less to claim it than to bestow. [. . .]

The nature of the fault, so far as it exists in the painters themselves, may perhaps best be discerned by comparing them with a man who went not far beyond them in his general range of effort, but who did all his work in a wholly different temper—Hans Holbein.

The first great difference between them is of course in completeness of execution. Sir Joshua's and Gainsborough's work, at its best, is only magnificent sketching; giving indeed, in places, a perfection of result unattainable by other methods, and possessing always a charm of grace and power exclusively its own; yet, in its slightness addressing itself, purposefully, to the casual glance, and common thought—eager to arrest the passer-by, but careless to detain him; or detaining him, if at all, by an unexplained enchantment, not by continuance of teaching, or development of idea. But the work of Holbein is true and thorough; accomplished, in the highest as the most literal sense, with a calm entireness of unaffected resolution, which sacrifices nothing, forgets nothing, and fears nothing.

—"Sir Joshua and Holbein" (1860)

★

{"what [Holbein] sees, he sees with his whole soul"}

Respecting the advantage, or the contrary, of so great earnestness in drawing a portrait of an uncelebrated person, we raise at present no debate: I only wish the reader to note this quality of earnestness, as entirely separating Holbein from Sir Joshua,—raising him into another sphere of intellect. For here is no question of mere difference in style or in power, none of minuteness or largeness. It is a question of Entireness. Holbein is *complete* in intellect: what he sees, he sees with his whole soul: what he paints, he paints with his whole might. Sir Joshua sees partially, slightly, tenderly—catches the flying lights of things, the momentary glooms: paints also partially, tenderly, never with half his strength; content with uncertain visions, insecure delights; the truth not precious nor significant to him, only pleasing; falsehood also pleasurable, even useful on occasion—must, however, be discreetly touched, just enough to make all men noble, all women lovely [. . .].

—"Sir Joshua and Holbein" (1860)

★

{"the mind of man never invented a greater thing than the form of man, animated by faithful life"}

It is impossible to find the three motives in fairer balance and harmony than in our own Reynolds. He rejoices in showing you his skill; and those of you who succeed in learning what painter's work really is, will one day rejoice also, even to laughter—that highest laughter which springs of pure delight, in watching the fortitude and the fire of a hand which strikes forth its will upon the canvas as easily as the wind strikes it on the sea. He rejoices in all abstract beauty and rhythm and melody of design; he will never give you a colour that is not lovely, nor a shade that is unnecessary, nor a line that is ungraceful. But all his power and all his invention are held by him subordinate,—and the more obediently because of their nobleness,—to his true leading purpose of setting before you such likeness of the living presence of an English gentleman or an English lady, as shall be worthy of being looked upon for ever.

But farther, you remember, I hope—for I said it in a way that I thought would shock you a little, that you might remember it—my statement, that art had never done more than this, never more than given the likeness of a noble human being. Not only so, but it very seldom does so much as this; and the best pictures that exist of the great schools are all portraits, or groups of portraits, often of very simple and no wise noble persons. You may have much more brilliant and impressive qualities in imaginative pictures; you may have figures scattered like clouds, or garlanded like flowers; you may have light and shade, as of a tempest, and colour, as of the rainbow; but all that is child's play to the great men, though it is astonishment to us. Their real strength is tried to the utmost, and as far as I know, it is never elsewhere brought out so thoroughly, as in painting one man or woman, and the soul that was in them; nor that always the highest soul, but often only a thwarted one that was capable of height; or perhaps not even that, but faultful and poor, yet seen through, to the poor best of it, by the masterful sight. So that in order to put before you [. . .] the best art possible, I am obliged, even from the very strongest men, to take portraits, before I take the idealism. Nay, whatever is best in the great compositions themselves has depended on portraiture; and the study necessary to enable you to understand invention will also convince you that the mind of man never invented a greater thing than the form of man, animated by faithful life. Every attempt to refine or exalt such healthy humanity has weakened or caricatured it; or else consists only in giving it, to please our fancy, the wings of birds, or the eyes of antelopes. Whatever is truly great in either Greek or Christian art, is also restrictedly human; and even the raptures of the redeemed souls who enter, "celestemente ballando,"[19] the gate of Angelico's Paradise, were seen first in the terrestrial, yet most pure, mirth of Florentine maidens.

—*Lectures on Art*, "The Relation of Art to Use" (1870)

★

[. . .] all inferior artists are continually trying to escape from the necessity of sound work, and either indulging themselves in their delights in subject, or pluming themselves on their noble motives for attempting what they cannot perform; (and observe, by the way, that a great deal of what is mistaken for conscientious motive is nothing but a very pestilent, because very subtle, condition of vanity); whereas the great men always understand at once that the first morality of a painter, as of everybody else, is to know his business; and so earnest are they in this, that many, whose lives you would think, by the results of their work, had been passed in strong emotion, have in reality subdued themselves, though capable of the very strongest passions, into a calm as absolute as that of a deeply sheltered mountain lake, which reflects every agitation of the clouds in the sky, and every change of the shadows on the hills, but is itself motionless.

—*Lectures on Art*, "The Relation of Art to Morals" (1870)

★

{Of Michelangelo versus Tintoretto, who "works in the consciousness of supreme strength"}

Hitherto, I have massed, necessarily, but most unjustly, Michael Angelo and Tintoret together, because of their common relation to the art of others. I shall now proceed to distinguish the qualities of their own. And first as to the general temper of the two men.

Nearly every existing work by Michael Angelo is an attempt to execute something beyond his power, coupled with a fevered desire that his power may be acknowledged. He is always matching himself

[19] Ruskin is quoting from Giorgio Vasari's "Life of Beato Angelico da Fiesole": "dancing heavenly" or, in Mrs. Jonathan's 1898 translation, "triumphal dance." [I beati si veggiono entrare *celestemente ballando* per la porta del paradiso.]

either against the Greeks whom he cannot rival, or against rivals whom he cannot forget. He is proud, yet not proud enough to be at peace; melancholy, yet not deeply enough to be raised above petty pain; and strong beyond all his companion workmen, yet never strong enough to command his temper, or limit his aims.

Tintoret, on the contrary, works in the consciousness of supreme strength, which cannot be wounded by neglect, and is only to be thwarted by time and space. He knows precisely all that art can accomplish under given conditions; determines absolutely how much of what can be done he will himself for the moment choose to do; and fulfills his purpose with as much ease as if, through his human body, were working the great forces of nature. Not that he is ever satisfied with what he has done, as vulgar and feeble artists are satisfied. He falls short of his ideal, more than any other man; but not more than is necessary; and is content to fall short of it to that degree, as he is content that his figures, however well painted, do not move nor speak. He is also entirely unconcerned respecting the satisfaction of the public. He neither cares to display his strength to them, nor convey his ideas to them; when he finishes his work, it is because he is in the humor to do so; and the sketch which a meaner painter would have left incomplete to show how cleverly it was begun, Tintoret simply leaves because he has done as much of it as he likes.

Both Raphael and Michael Angelo are thus, in the most vital of all points, separate from the great Venetian. They are always in dramatic attitudes, and always appealing to the public for praise. They are the leading athletes in the gymnasium of the arts; and the crowd of the circus cannot take its eyes away from them, while the Venetian walks or rests with the simplicity of a wild animal; is scarcely noticed in his occasionally swifter motion; when he springs, it is to please himself; and so calmly, that no one thinks of estimating the distance covered. I do not praise him wholly in this. I praise him only for the well-founded pride, infinitely nobler than Michael Angelo's. You do not hear of Tintoret's putting any one into hell because they had found fault with his work. Tintoret would as soon have thought of putting a dog into hell for laying his paws on it. But he is to be blamed in this—that he thinks as little of the pleasure of the public, as of their opinion. A great painter's business is to do what the public ask of him, in the way that shall be helpful and instructive to them. His relation to them is exactly that of a tutor to a child; he is not to defer to their judgment, but he is carefully to form it;—not to consult their pleasure for his own sake, but to consult it much for theirs. It was scarcely, however, possible that this should be the case between Tintoret and his Venetians; he could not paint for the people, and in some respects he was happily protected by his subordination to the Senate. Raphael and Michael Angelo lived in a world of court intrigue, in which it was impossible to escape petty irritation, or refuse themselves the pleasure of mean victory. But Tintoret and Titian, even at the height of their reputation, practically lived as craftsmen in their workshops, and sent in samples of their wares, not to be praised or caviled at, but to be either taken or refused.

—*Arata Pentelici*, "The Relation between Michael Angelo and Tintoret" (1870)

★

{Of Michelangelo: "All that shadowing, storming, and coiling of his [. . .] is mere stage decoration"}

You are accustomed to think the figures of Michael Angelo sublime—because they are dark, and colossal, and involved, and mysterious—because in a word, they look sometimes like shadows, and sometimes like mountains, and sometimes like specters, but never like human beings. Believe me, yet once more, in what I told you long since—man can invent nothing nobler than humanity. He cannot raise his form into anything better than God made it, by giving it either the flight of birds or strength of beasts, by enveloping it in mist, or heaping it into multitude. Your pilgrim must look like a pilgrim in a straw hat, or you will not make him into one with cockle and nimbus; an angel must look like an angel on the ground, as well as in the air; and the much-denounced pre-Raphaelite faith that a saint cannot look saintly unless he has thin legs, is not more absurd than Michael Angelo's, that a Sybil cannot look Sibylline unless she has thick ones.

All that shadowing, storming, and coiling of his, when you look into it, is mere stage decoration, and that of a vulgar kind. Light is, in reality, more awful than darkness—modesty more majestic than strength; and there is truer sublimity in the sweet joy of a child, or the sweet virtue of a maiden, than in the strength of Antæus, or thunder-clouds of Ætna. Now, though in nearly all his greater pictures, Tintoret is entirely carried away by his sympathy with Michael Angelo, and conquers him in his own field;—outflies him in motion, outnumbers him in multitude, outwits him in fancy, and outflames him in rage,—he can be just as gentle as he is strong: and that Paradise, though it is the largest picture in the world, without any question, is also the thoughtfulest, and most precious.

The Thoughtfulest!—it would be saying but little, as far as Michael Angelo is concerned.

—*Arata Pentelici*, "The Relation between Michael Angelo and Tintoret" (1870)

★

{"There is no other human skill so great or so wonderful as the skill of fine oil-painting"}

You have often heard quoted the saying of Michael Angelo, that oil-painting was only fit for women and children. He said so, simply because he had neither the skill to lay a single touch of good oil-painting, nor the patience to overcome even its elementary difficulties.

And it is one of my reasons for the choice of subject in this concluding lecture on Sculpture, that I may, with direct reference to this much quoted saying of Michael Angelo, make the positive statement to you, that oil-painting is the Art of arts; that it is sculpture, drawing, and music, all in one, involving the technical dexterities of those three several arts; that is to say—the decision and strength of the stroke of the chisel;—the balanced distribution of appliance of that force necessary for graduation in light and shade;—and the passionate felicity of rightly multiplied actions, all unerring, which on an instrument produce right sound, and on canvas, living colour. There is no other human skill so great or so wonderful as the skill of fine oil-painting; and there is no other art whose results are so absolutely permanent. Music is gone as soon as produced—marble discolours,—fresco fades,—glass darkens or decomposes—painting alone, well guarded, is practically everlasting.

—*Arata Pentelici*, "The Relation Between Michael Angelo and Tintoret" (1870)

★

{Botticelli "has the power of Tintoret, with the virtue of Angelico"}

All great artists may be classified under three heads—Colourists, Delineators, Chiaroscurists; that is to say, they all possess one of these three qualities pre-eminently, though they possess all three in a greater or lesser degree, the greatest artists having almost as much of the other two qualities as of their pre-eminent one. Of Chiaroscurists, the chief is Tintoret. He learned of painters only, Titian and Giorgione. He had the pencil or the brush in his hand from his youth; his favourite colours were black and white; he painted with a broad brush. There is no chiaroscuro like Tintoret's; but under it is colour as subtle as Angelico's, though subordinate. Of Colourists, the chief is Angelico. He learned to paint by writing; he was taught by a Dominican illuminator, and is himself the chief illuminator of the world. There is no colour like Angelico's; but under it is chiaroscuro as subtle as Tintoret's, though subordinate. His jewel painting was not enough leaned on; a single amethyst in the robe of the Madonna would have taken me half a day to copy, in the gradations of its transparently flushed purple. Of Delineators, the chief is Botticelli. Taught by a goldsmith, he learnt by gold-beating and engraving, and is himself a master goldsmith and engraver. Ghirlandajo is a goldsmith selling plated goods; Botticelli's is pure gold tried in the fire, and engraved as Bezaleel and Aholiab engraved. There is no drawing like Botticelli's; but under it is colour and chiaroscuro as subtle as Angelico's and Tintoret's, but subordinate.

He draws first with the point of the brush; but, like all masters who begin with the point, he soon gets a wonderful power with the side of it, and we find leaves drawn by Botticelli with a single stroke,—the point of the brush beginning, and the brush opening out as it goes. Angelico entered a convent at twenty, painting and living only for the poor, and called "Beatus." Botticelli lived amidst the concourse of Florence, admiring all earthly beauty, himself untainted by it. He is in one the most learned theologian, the most perfect artist, and the most kind gentleman whom Florence produced. He knows all that Dante knew of theology, and much more; and he is the only unerring, unfearing, and to this day trustworthy and true preacher of the reformed doctrine of the Church of Christ. As an artist he is incomparable. He has the power of Tintoret, with the virtue of Angelico; and he is such a gentleman that he interprets all things with charity in days of grievous guilt, spends himself and all he has in the passionate service of men and of God, and dies in Florence, having given not half but all his goods to the poor—engraving the triumph of the faith of Savonarola.

—*The Aesthetic and Mathematic Schools of Art in Florence: Lectures Given Before the University of Oxford in Michaelmas Term, 1874*, "Botticelli" (1874)

★

{Giotto "defines, explains, and exalts, every sweet incident of human nature"}

Domestic and monastic. He was the first of Italians—the first of Christians—who *equally* knew the virtue of both lives; and who was able to show it in the sight of men of all ranks,—from the prince to the shepherd; and of all powers,—from the wisest philosopher to the simplest child.

For, note the way in which the new gift of painting, bequeathed to him by his great master, strengthened his hands. Before Cimabue, no beautiful rendering of human form was possible; and the rude or formal types of the Lombard and Byzantine, though they would serve in the tumult of the chase, or as the recognized symbols of creed, could not represent personal and domestic character. Faces with goggling eyes and rigid lips might be endured with ready help of imagination, for gods, angels, saints, or hunters—or for anybody else in scenes of recognized legend, but would not serve for pleasant portraiture of one's own self—or of the incidents of gentle, actual life. And even Cimabue did not venture to leave the sphere of conventionally reverenced dignity. He still painted—though beautifully—only the Madonna, and the St. Joseph, and the Christ. These he made living,—Florence asked no more: and "Credette Cimabue nella pintura tener lo campo." But Giotto came from the field, and saw with his simple eyes a lowlier worth. And he painted—the Madonna, and St. Joseph, and the Christ,—yes, by all means if you choose to call them so, but essentially,—Mamma, Papa, and the Baby. And all Italy threw up its cap,—"Ora ha Giotto il grido."[20]

For he defines, explains, and exalts, every sweet incident of human nature; and makes dear to daily life every mystic imagination of natures greater than our own. He reconciles, while he intensifies, every virtue of domestic and monastic thought. He makes the simplest household duties sacred, and the highest religious passions serviceable and just.

—*Mornings in Florence*, "The Second Morning. The Golden Gate" (1875–1877)

[20] Ruskin is quoting from Dante's *Purgatorio*, Canto 11: "In painting Cimabue thought that he / Should hold the field, now Giotto has the cry [. . .]." Translation by Henry Wadsworth Longfellow.

★

{"The only absolute masters of light and shade are those who never make you *think* of light and shade, more than Nature herself does"}

[. . .] you probably have been beguiled, before now, into admiring Raphael's *Transfiguration*, in which everybody's faces and limbs are half black; and into supposing Rembrandt a master of chiaroscuro, because he can paint a vigorous portrait with a black dab under the nose!

Both Raphael and Rembrandt *are* masters, indeed; but neither of them masters of light and shade, in treatment of which the first is always false, and the second always vulgar. The only absolute masters of light and shade are those who never make you *think* of light and shade, more than Nature herself does.

—*The Laws of Fesole*, "Of Light and Shade" (1877)

Colour

{"great power over colour is always a sign of large general art-intellect"}

IF HE CAN colour, he is a painter, though he can do nothing else; if he cannot colour, he is no painter, though he may do everything else. But it is, in fact, impossible, if he can colour, but that he should be able to do more; for a faithful study of colour will always give power over form, though the most intense study of form will give no power over colour. The man who can see all the greys, and reds, and purples in a peach, will paint the peach rightly round, and rightly altogether; but the man who has only studied its roundness, may not see its purples and greys, and if he does not, will never get it to look like a peach; so that great power over colour is always a sign of large general art-intellect. Expression of the most subtle kind can be often reached by the slight studies of caricaturists; sometimes elaborated by the toil of the dull, and sometimes by the sentiment of the feeble, but to colour well requires real talent and earnest study, and to colour perfectly is the rarest and most precious power an artist can possess. Every other gift may be erroneously cultivated, but this will guide to all healthy, natural, and forcible truth; the student may be led into folly by philosophers, and into falsehood by purists; but he is always safe if he holds the hand of a colourist.

—*Modern Painters*, Vol. IV, "Of Turnerian Light" (1856)

*

{"when we first look at a subject, we get a glimpse of some of the greatest truths about it"}

[. . .] we find the greatest artists mainly divided into two groups,—those who paint principally with respect to local colour, headed by

Paul Veronese, Titian, and Turner; and those who paint principally with reference to light and shade irrespective of colour, headed by Leonardo da Vinci, Rembrandt, and Raphael. The noblest members of each of these classes introduce the element proper to the other class, in a subordinate way. Paul Veronese introduces a subordinate light and shade, and Leonardo introduces a subordinate local colour. The main difference is, that with Leonardo, Rembrandt, and Raphael, vast masses of the picture are lost in comparatively colourless (dark, grey, or brown) shadow; these painters beginning with the lights, and going down to blackness; but with Veronese, Titian, and Turner, the whole picture is like the rose,—glowing with colour in the shadows, and rising into paler and more delicate hues, or masses of whiteness, in the lights; they having begun with the shadows, and gone up to whiteness.

The colourists have in this respect one disadvantage, and three advantages. The disadvantage is, that between their less violent hues, it is not possible to draw all the forms which can be represented by the exaggerated shadow of the chiaroscurists, and therefore a slight tendency to flatness is always characteristic of the greater colourists, as opposed to Leonardo or Rembrandt. When the form of some single object is to be given, and its subtleties are to be rendered to the utmost, the Leonardesque manner of drawing is often very noble. It is generally adopted by Albert [Albrecht] Dürer in his engravings, and is very useful, when employed by a thorough master, in many kinds of engraving; but it is an utterly false method of study, as we shall see presently.

Of the three advantages possessed by the colourists over the chiaroscurists, the first is, that they have in the greater portions of their pictures absolute truth, while the chiaroscurists have no absolute truth anywhere. With the colourists the shadows are right; the lights untrue: but with the chiaroscurists lights and shadows are both untrue. The second advantage is, that also the relations of colour are broader and vaster with the colourists than the chiaroscurists. Take, for example, that piece of drapery studied by Leonardo, in the Louvre, with white lights and black shadows. Ask yourself, first, whether the real drapery was black or white. If white, then its high lights are rightly white; but its folds being black, it could not as a mass be distinguished from the black or dark objects in its neighborhood. But the fact is, that a white cloth or handkerchief always is distinguished in daylight, as a whole white thing, from all that is coloured about it: we see at once that there is a white piece of stuff, and a red, or green, or grey one near it, as the case may be: and this relation of the white object to other objects not white, Leonardo has wholly deprived himself of the power of expressing; while, if the cloth were black or dark, much more has he erred by making its lights white. In either case, he has missed the large relation of mass to mass, for the sake of the small one of fold to fold. And this is more or less the case with all chiaroscurists; with all painters, that is to say, who endeavor in their studies of objects to get rid of the idea of colour, and give the abstract shade. They invariably exaggerate the shadows, not with respect to the thing itself, but with respect to all around it; and they exaggerate the lights also, by leaving pure white for the high light of what in reality is grey, rose-coloured, or, in some way, not white.

This method of study, being peculiarly characteristic of the Roman and Florentine schools, and associated with very accurate knowledge of form and expression, has gradually got to be thought by a large body of artists the grand way of study; an idea which has been fostered all the more because it was an unnatural way, and therefore thought to be a philosophical one. Almost the first idea of a child, or of a simple person looking at anything, is, that it is a red, or a black, or a green, or a white thing. Nay, say the artists; that is an unphilosophical and barbarous view of the matter. Red and white are mere vulgar appearances; look farther into the matter, and you will see such and such wonderful other appearances. Abstract those, they are the heroic, epic, historic, and generally eligible appearances. And acting on this grand principle, they draw flesh white, leaves white, ground white, everything white in the light, and everything black in the shade—and think themselves wise. But, the longer I live, the more ground I see to hold in high honor a certain sort of childishness or innocent susceptibility. Generally speaking, I find that when we first look at a subject, we get a glimpse of some of the greatest truths about it: as we look longer, our vanity, and false reasoning, and half-knowledge, lead us into various wrong opinions; but as we look longer still, we gradually return to our first impressions, only with a full understanding of their mystical and innermost reasons; and of much beyond and beside them, not then known to us, now added (partly as a foundation, partly as a corollary) to what at first we felt or saw. It is thus eminently in this matter of colour.

—*Modern Painters*, Vol. IV, "Of Turnerian Light" (1856)

★

{"The sky is not blue *colour* merely,—it is blue *fire*, and cannot be painted"}

[. . .] the sky is actually a brighter thing than white paper, by a certain number of degrees of light, scientifically determinable. In the same way, every other colour, or force of colour, is a fixed thing, not dependent on sensation, but numerically representable with as much exactitude as a degree of heat by a thermometer. And of these hues, that of open sky is one not producible by human art. The sky is not blue *colour* merely,—it is blue *fire*, and cannot be painted.

Next, observe, this blue fire has in it *white* fire; that is, it has white clouds, as much brighter than itself as *it* is brighter than the white paper. So, then, above this azure light, we have another equally exalted step of white light. Supposing the value of the light of the pure white paper represented by the number 10, then that of the blue sky will be (approximately) about 20, and of the white clouds 30.

But look at the white clouds carefully, and it will be seen they are not all of the same white; parts of them are quite grey compared with other parts, and they are as full of passages of light and shade as if they were of solid earth. Nevertheless, their most deeply shaded part is that already so much lighter than the blue sky, which has brought us up to our number 30, and all these high lights of white are some 10 degrees above that, or, to white paper, as 40 to 10. And now if you look from the blue sky and white clouds towards the sun, you will find that this cloud white, which is four times as white as white paper, is quite dark and lightless compared with those silver clouds that burn nearer the sun itself, which you cannot gaze upon,—an infinite of brightness. How will you estimate that?

And yet to express all this, we have but our poor white paper after all. We must not talk too proudly of our "truths" of art; I am afraid we shall have to let a good deal of black fallacy into it, at the best.

Well, of the sun, and of the silver clouds, we will not talk for the present. But this principal fact we have learned by our experiment with the white paper, that, taken all in all, the calm sky, with such light and shade as are in it, is brighter than the earth; brighter than the whitest thing on earth which has not, at the moment of comparison, heaven's own direct light on it. Which fact it is generally one of the first objects of noble painters to render. I have already marked one part of their aim in doing so, namely, the expression of infinity; but the opposing of heavenly light to earth-darkness is another most important one; and of all ways of rendering a picture generally impressive, this is the simplest and surest. Make the sky calm and luminous, and raise against it dark trees, mountains, or towers, or any other substantial and terrestrial thing, in bold outline, and the mind accepts the assertion of this great and solemn truth with thankfulness.

—*Modern Painters*, Vol. IV, "Of Turnerian Light" (1856)

★

{"the whole art of Painting consists merely in perceiving the shape and depth of these patches of colour"}

The perception of solid Form is entirely a matter of experience. We see nothing but flat colours; and it is only by a series of experiments that we find out that a stain of black or gray indicates the dark side of a solid substance, or that a faint hue indicates that the object in which it appears is far away. The whole technical power of painting depends on our recovery of what may be called the *innocence of the eye*; that is to say, of a sort of childish perception of these flat stains of colour, merely as such, without consciousness of what they signify,—as a blind man would see them if suddenly gifted with sight. [. . .]

Now, a highly accomplished artist has always reduced himself as nearly as possible to this condition of infantine sight. He sees the colours of nature exactly as they are, and therefore perceives at once in the sunlighted grass the precise relation between the two colours that form its shade and light. To him it does not seem shade and light, but bluish green barred with gold.

Strive, therefore, first of all, to convince yourself of this great fact about sight. This, in your hand, which you know by experience and touch to be a book, is to your eye nothing but a patch of white, variously gradated and spotted; this other thing near you, which by experience you know to be a table, is to your eye only a patch of brown, variously darkened and veined; and so on: and the whole art of Painting consists merely in perceiving the shape and depth of these patches of colour, and putting patches of the same size, depth, and shape on canvas. The only obstacle to the success of painting is, that many of the real colours are brighter and paler than it is possible to put on canvas: we must put darker ones to represent them.

—*The Elements of Drawing*, "On First Practice" (1857)

★

{"If the colour is wrong, everything is wrong"}

And, though of course you should always give as much form to your subject as your attention to its colour will admit of, remember that the whole value of what you are about depends, in a coloured sketch, on the colour merely. If the colour is wrong, everything is wrong: just as, if you are singing, and sing false notes, it does not matter how true the words are. If you sing at all, you must sing sweetly; and if you colour at all, you must colour rightly. Give up all the form, rather than the slightest part of the colour: just as, if you felt yourself in danger of a false note, you would give up the word and sing a meaningless sound, if you felt that so you could save the note. Never mind though your houses are all tumbling down, though your clouds are mere blots, and your trees mere knobs, and your sun and moon like crooked sixpences, so only that trees, clouds, houses, and sun or moon, are of the right colours.

—*The Elements of Drawing,* "Of Colour and Composition" (1857)

★

{"The art of painting [. . .] consists in laying on the least possible colour that will produce the required result"}

The law concerning colour is very strange, very noble, in some sense almost awful. In every given touch laid on canvas, if one grain of the colour is inoperative, and does not take its full part in producing the hue, the hue will be imperfect. The grain of colour which does not work is dead. It infects all about it with its death. It must be got quit of, or the touch is spoiled. We acknowledge this instinctively in our use of the phrases "dead colour," "killed colour," "foul colour." Those words are, in some sort, literally true. If more colour is put on than is necessary, a heavy touch when a light one would have been enough, the quantity of colour that was not wanted, and is overlaid by the rest, is as dead, and it pollutes the rest. There will be no good in the touch.

The art of painting, properly so called, consists in laying on the least possible colour that will produce the required result, and this measurement, in all the ultimate, that is to say, the principal, operations of colouring, is so delicate that not one human hand in a million has the required lightness. The final touch of any painter properly so named, of Correggio—Titian—Turner—or Reynolds—

would be always quite invisible to any one watching the progress of the work, the films of hue being laid thinner than the depths of the grooves in mother-of-pearl. The work may be swift, apparently careless, nay, to the painter himself almost unconscious. Great painters are so organized that they do their best work without effort: but analyze the touches afterwards, and you will find the structure and depth of the colour laid mathematically demonstrable to be of literally infinite fineness, the last touches passing away at their edges by untraceable gradation. The very essence of a master's work may thus be removed by a picture-cleaner in ten minutes.

—*The Two Paths*, Appendix 4, "Subtlety of Hand" (1858)

*

{"Any other but a Venetian would have put a complete piece of white paint over the dress"}

This is, as far as it can be expressed in few words, the right, or Venetian way of painting; but it is incapable of absolute definition, for it depends on the scale, the material, and the nature of the object represented, how much a great painter will do with his first colour; or how many after processes he will use. Very often the first colour, richly blended and worked into, is also the last; sometimes it wants a glaze only to modify it; sometimes an entirely different colour above it. Turner's storm-blues, for instance, were produced by a black ground, with opaque blue, mixed with white, struck over it. The amount of detail given in the first colour will also depend on convenience. For instance, if a jewel fastens a fold of dress, a Venetian will lay probably a piece of the jewel colour in its place at the time he draws the fold; but if the jewel falls upon the dress, he will paint the folds only in the ground colour, and the jewel afterwards. For in the first case his hand must pause, at any rate, where the fold is fastened; so that he may as well mark the colour of the gem: but he would have to check his hand in the sweep with which he drew the drapery, if he painted a jewel that fell upon it with the first colour. So far, however, as he can possibly use the under colour, he will, in whatever he has to superimpose. There is a pretty little instance of such economical work in the painting of the pearls on the breast of the elder princess, in our best Paul Veronese (*Family of Darius*). The lowest is about the size of a small hazel-nut, and falls on her rose-red dress. Any other but a Venetian would have put a complete piece of white paint over the dress, for the whole pearl, and painted into that the colours of the stone. But Veronese knows beforehand that all the dark side of the pearl will reflect the red of the dress. He will not put white over the red, only to put red over the white again. He leaves the actual dress for the dark side of the pearl, and with two small separate touches, one white, another brown, places its high light and shadow. This he does with perfect care and calm; but in two decisive seconds. There is no dash, nor display, nor hurry, nor error. The exactly right thing is done in the exactly right place, and not one atom of colour, nor moment of time spent vainly. Look close at the two touches,—you wonder what they mean. Retire six feet from the picture—the pearl is there!

—*Modern Painters*, Vol. V, "The Law of Perfectness" (1860)

*

{"Painting is playing on a colour-violin, seventy-times-seven stringed, and inventing your tune as you play it!"}

You will continually hear artists disputing about grounds, glazings, vehicles, varnishes, transparencies, opacities, oleaginousnesses. All that talk is as idle as the east wind. Get a flat surface that won't crack, some coloured substance that will stick upon it, and remain always of the colour it was when you put it on, and a pig's bristle or two, wedged in a stick; and if you can't paint, you are no painter; and had better not talk about the art.

The one thing you have to learn—the one power truly called that of "painting"—is to lay on any coloured substance, whatever its consistence may be, (from mortar to ether,) at once, of the exact tint you want, in the exact form you want, and in the exact quantity you want. That is painting.

Now, you are well aware that to play on the violin well, requires some practice. Painting is playing on a colour-violin, seventy-times-seven stringed, and inventing your tune as you play it! That is the easy, simple, straightforward business you have to learn. Here is your catgut and your mahogany,—better or worse quality of both of course there may be,—Cremona tone, and so on, to be discussed with due care, in due time;—you cannot paint miniature on the sail of a fishing-boat, nor do the fine work with hog's bristles that you can with camel's hair:—all these catgut and bristle questions shall have their place; but, the primary question of all is—can you play?

Perfectly, you never can, but by birth-gift. The entirely first-rate musicians and painters are born, like Mercury;—their words are music, and their touch is gold; sound and colour wait on them from their youth; and no practice will ever enable other human creatures to do any thing like them. The most favorable conditions, the most docile and apt temper, and the unwearied practice of life, will never enable any painter of merely average human capacity to lay a single touch like Gainsborough, Velásquez, Tintoret, or Luini. But to understand that the matter must still depend on practice as well as on genius,—that painting is not one whit less, but more, difficult than playing on an instrument,—and that your care as a student, on the whole, is not to be given to the quality of your piano, but of your touch,—this is the great fact which I have to teach you respecting colour; this is the root of all excellent doing and perceiving.

And you will be utterly amazed, when once you begin to feel what colour means, to find how many qualities which appear to result from peculiar method and material do indeed depend only on loveliness of execution; and how divine the law of nature is, which has so connected the immortality of beauty with patience of industry, that by precision and rightness of laborious art you may at last literally command the rainbow to stay, and forbid the sun to set.

—*The Laws of Fesole*, "Of the Twelve Zodiacal Colours" (1877)

Definitions

{"the art is greatest, which conveys to the mind of the spectator [. . .] the greatest number of the greatest ideas"}

[. . .] IF I SAY that the greatest picture is that which conveys to the mind of the spectator the greatest number of the greatest ideas, I have a definition which will include as subjects of comparison every pleasure which art is capable of conveying. If I were to say, on the contrary, that the best picture was that which most closely imitated nature, I should assume that art could only please by imitating nature, and I should cast out of the pale of criticism those parts of works of art which are not imitative, that is to say, intrinsic beauties of colour and form, and those works of art wholly, which, like the arabesques of Raffaelle in the Loggias, are not imitative at all. Now I want a definition of art wide enough to include all its varieties of aim: I do not say therefore that the art is greatest which gives most pleasure, because perhaps there is some art whose end is to teach, and not to please. I do not say that the art is greatest which teaches us most, because perhaps there is some art whose end is to please, and not to teach. I do not say that the art is greatest which imitates best, because perhaps there is some art whose end is to create, and not to imitate. But I say that the art is greatest, which conveys to the mind of the spectator, by any means whatsoever, the greatest number of the greatest ideas, and I call an idea great in proportion as it is received by a higher faculty of the mind, and as it more fully occupies, and in occupying, exercises and exalts, the faculty by which it is received.

If this then be the definition of great art, that of a great artist naturally follows. He is the greatest artist who has embodied, in the sum of his works, the greatest number of the greatest ideas.

—*Modern Painters*, Vol. I, "Introductory" (1843)

★

{"imagination is a voluntary summoning of the conceptions of things absent or impossible"}

[. . .] it might be at first thought that the whole kingdom of imagination was one of deception also. Not so: the action of the imagination is a voluntary summoning of the conceptions of things absent or impossible; and the pleasure and nobility of the imagination partly consist in its knowledge and contemplation of them as such, i.e. in the knowledge of their actual absence or impossibility at the moment of their apparent presence or reality. When the imagination deceives it becomes madness. It is a noble faculty so long as it confesses its own ideality; when it ceases to confess this, it is insanity. All the difference lies in the fact of the confession, in there being *no* deception. It is necessary to our rank as spiritual creatures, that we should be able to invent and to behold what is not; and to our rank as moral creatures that we should know and confess at the same time that it is not.

Again, it might be thought, and has been thought, that the whole art of painting is nothing else than an endeavor to deceive. Not so: it is, on the contrary, a statement of certain facts, in the clearest possible way. For instance: I desire to give an account of a mountain or of a rock; I begin by telling its shape. But words will not do this distinctly, and I draw its shape, and say, "This was its shape." Next: I would fain represent its colour; but words will not do this either, and I dye the paper, and say, "This was its colour." Such a process may be carried on until the scene appears to exist, and a high pleasure may be taken in its apparent existence. This is a communicated act of imagination, but no lie. The lie can consist only in an *assertion* of its existence (which is never for one instant made, implied, or believed), or else in false statements of forms and colours (which are, indeed, made and believed to our great loss, continually). And observe, also, that so degrading a thing is deception in even the approach and appearance of it, that all painting which even reaches the mark of apparent realization, is degraded in so doing. I have enough insisted on this point in another place.

—*The Seven Lamps of Architecture*, "Conceptions of Things Absent or Impossible" (1849)

★

{"No machine yet contrived [. . .] will ever equal the fine machinery of the human fingers"}

It would be well if all students would keep clearly in their mind the real distinction between those words which we use so often, "Manufacture," "Art," and "Fine Art." "MANUFACTURE" is, according to the etymology and right use of the word, "the making of anything by hands,"—directly or indirectly, with or without the help of instruments or machines. Anything proceeding from the hand of man is manufacture; but it must have proceeded from his hand only, acting mechanically, and uninfluenced at the moment by direct intelligence.

Then, secondly, ART is the operation of the hand and the intelligence of man together; there is an art of making machinery; there is an art of building ships; an art of making carriages; and so on. All these, properly called Arts, but not Fine Arts, are pursuits in which the hand of man and his head go together, working at the same instant.

Then FINE ART is that in which the hand, the head, and the *heart* of man go together. Recollect this triple group; it will help you to solve many difficult problems. And remember that though the hand must be at the bottom of everything, it must also go to the top of everything; for Fine Art must be produced by the hand of man in a much greater and clearer sense than manufacture is. Fine Art must always be produced by the subtlest of all machines, which is the human hand. No machine yet contrived, or hereafter contrivable, will ever equal the fine machinery of the human fingers. Thoroughly perfect art is that which proceeds from the heart, which involves all the noble emotions;—associates with these the head, yet as inferior to the heart; and the hand, yet as inferior to the heart and head; and thus brings out the whole man.

—*The Two Paths*, "The Unity of Art" (1858)

★

{"the greatest art yet produced has been decorative"}

Observe, then, first—the only essential distinction between Decorative and other art is the being fitted for a fixed place; and in that place, related, either in subordination or command, to the effect of other pieces of art. And all the greatest art which the world has produced is thus fitted for a place, and subordinated to a purpose. There is no existing highest-order art but is decorative. The best sculpture yet produced has been the decoration of a temple front—the best painting, the decoration of a room. Raphael's best doing is merely the wall-colouring of a suite of apartments in the Vatican, and his cartoons were made for tapestries. Correggio's best doing is the decoration of two small church cupolas at Parma; Michael Angelo's of a ceiling in the Pope's private chapel; Tintoret's, of a ceiling and side wall belonging to a charitable society at Venice; while Titian and Veronese threw out their noblest thoughts, not even on the inside, but on the outside of the common brick and plaster walls of Venice.

Get rid, then, at once of any idea of Decorative art being a degraded or a separate kind of art. Its nature or essence is simply its being fitted for a definite place; and, in that place, forming part of a great and harmonious whole, in companionship with other art; and so far from this being a degradation to it—so far from Decorative art being inferior to other art because it is fixed to a spot—on the whole it may be considered as rather a piece of degradation that it should be portable. Portable art—independent of all place—is for the most part ignoble art. Your little Dutch landscape, which you put over your sideboard to-day, and between the windows tomorrow, is a far more contemptible piece of work than the extents of field and forest with which Benozzo has made green and beautiful the once melancholy arcade of the Campo Santo at Pisa; and the wild boar of silver which you use for a seal, or lock into a velvet case, is little likely to be so noble a beast as the bronze boar who foams forth the fountain from under his tusks in the market-place of Florence. It is, indeed, possible that the portable picture or image may be first-rate of its kind, but it is not first-rate because it is portable; nor are Titian's frescoes less than first-rate because they are fixed; nay, very frequently the highest compliment you can pay to a cabinet picture is to say—"It is as grand as a fresco."

—*The Two Paths*, "Modern Manufacturing and Design" (1858)

★

{"There have only yet appeared in the world three schools of perfect art"}

Review for yourselves the history of art, and you will find this to be a manifest certainty, that *no great school ever yet existed which had not for primal aim the representation of some natural fact as truly as possible.* There have only yet appeared in the world three schools of perfect art—schools, that is to say, that did their work as well as it seems possible to do it. These are the Athenian, Florentine, and Venetian. The Athenian proposed to itself the perfect representation of the form of the human body. It strove to do that as well as it could; it did that as well as it can be done; and all its greatness was founded upon and involved in that single and honest effort. The Florentine school proposed to itself the perfect expression of human emotion—the showing of the effects of passion in the human face and gesture. I call this the Florentine school, because, whether you take Raphael for the culminating master of expressional art in Italy, or Leonardo, or Michael Angelo, you will find that the whole energy of the national effort which produced those masters had its root in Florence; not at Urbino or Milan. I say, then, this Florentine or leading Italian school proposed to itself human expression for its aim in natural truth; it strove to do that as well as it could—did it as well as it can be done—and all its greatness is rooted in that single and honest effort. Thirdly, the Venetian school proposed the representation of the effect of colour and shade on all things; chiefly on the human form. It tried to do that as well as it could—did it as well as it can be done—and all its greatness is founded on that single and honest effort.

Pray, do not leave this room without a perfectly clear holding of these three ideas. You may try them, and toss them about afterwards, as much as you like, to see if they'll bear shaking; but do let me put them well and plainly into your possession. Attach them to three works of art which you all have either seen or continually heard of. There's the (so-called) "Theseus" of the Elgin marbles. That represents the whole end and aim of the Athenian school—the natural form of the human body. All their conventional architecture—their graceful shaping and painting of pottery—whatsoever other art they practised—was dependent for its greatness on this sheet-anchor of central aim: true shape of living man. Then take, for your type of the Italian school, Raphael's *Disputa del Sacramento*; that will be an accepted type by everybody, and will involve no possibly questionable points: the Germans will admit it; the English academicians will admit it; and the English purists and pre-Raphaelites will admit it. Well, there you have the truth of human expression proposed as an aim. That is the way people look when they feel this or that—when they have this or that other mental character: are they devotional, thoughtful, affectionate, indignant, or inspired? are they prophets, saints, priests, or kings? then—whatsoever is truly thoughtful, affectionate, prophetic, priestly, kingly—*that* the Florentine school tried to discern, and show; *that* they have discerned and shown; and all their greatness is first fastened in their aim at this central truth—the open expression of the living human soul. Lastly, take Veronese's *Marriage in Cana* in the Louvre. There you have the most perfect representation possible of colour, and light, and shade, as they affect the external aspect of the human form, and its immediate accessories, architecture, furniture, and dress. This external aspect of noblest nature was the first aim of the Venetians, and all their greatness depended on their resolution to achieve, and their patience in achieving it.

—*The Two Paths*, "The Deteriorative Power of Conventional Art Over Nations" (1858)

Greatness

{"it is altogether impossible to foretell on what strange objects the strength of a great man will sometimes be concentrated"}

WE CANNOT SAY that a painter is great because he paints boldly, or paints delicately; because he generalizes or particularizes; because he loves detail, or because he disdains it. He is great if, by any of these means, he has laid open noble truths, or aroused noble emotions. It does not matter whether he paint the petal of a rose, or the chasms of a precipice, so that Love and Admiration attend him as he labors, and wait for ever upon his work. It does not matter whether he toil for months upon a few inches of his canvas, or cover a palace front with colour in a day, so only that it be with a solemn purpose that he has filled his heart with patience, or urged his hand to haste. And it does not matter whether he seek for his subjects among peasants or nobles, among the heroic or the simple, in courts or in fields, so only that he behold all things with a thirst for beauty, and a hatred of meanness and vice. There are, indeed, certain methods of representation which are usually adopted by the most active minds, and certain characters of subject usually delighted in by the noblest hearts; but it is quite possible, quite easy, to adopt the manner of painting without sharing the activity of mind, and to imitate the choice of subject without possessing the nobility of spirit; while, on the other hand, it is altogether impossible to foretell on what strange objects the strength of a great man will sometimes be concentrated, or by what strange means he will sometimes express himself. So that true criticism of art never can consist in the mere application of rules; it can be just only when it is founded on quick sympathy with the innumerable instincts and changeful efforts of human nature, chastened and guided by unchanging love of all things that God has created to be beautiful, and pronounced to be good.

—*Modern Painters*, Vol. III, "Of Realization" (1856)

★

{"everlasting difference is set between one man's capacity and another's"}

[. . .] greatness in art (as assuredly in all other things, but more distinctly in this than in most of them,) is not a teachable nor gainable thing, but *the expression of the mind of a God-made great man*; that teach, or preach, or labor as you will, everlasting difference is set between one man's capacity and another's; and that this God-given supremacy is the priceless thing, always just as rare in the world at one time as another.

—*Modern Painters*, Vol. III, "Of the Use of Pictures" (1856)

★

{"great men never know how or why they do things"}

If any man, seeing certain forms laid on the canvas, does by his reasoning power determine that certain changes wrought in them would mend or enforce them, that is not only uninventive, but contrary to invention, which must be the involuntary occurrence of certain forms or fancies to the mind in the order they are to be portrayed. Thus the knowing of rules and the exertion of judgment have a tendency to check and confuse the fancy in its flow; so that it will follow, that, in exact proportion as a master knows anything about rules of right and wrong, he is likely to be uninventive; and in exact proportion as he holds higher rank and has nobler inventive power, he will know less of rules; not despising them, but simply feeling that between him and them there is nothing in common,—that dreams cannot be ruled—that as they come, so they must be caught, and they cannot be caught in any other shape than that they come in; and that he might as well attempt to rule a rainbow into rectitude, or cut notches in a moth's wings to hold it by, as in any wise attempt to modify, by rule, the forms of the involuntary vision.

[. . .] The great men never know how or why they do things. They have no rules; cannot comprehend the nature of rules;—do not, usually, even know, in what they do, what is best or what is worst: to them it is all the same; something they cannot help saying or doing,—one piece of it as good as another, and none of it (it seems to *them*) worth much. The moment any man begins to talk about rules, in whatsoever art, you may know him for a second-rate man; and, if he talks about them *much*, he is a third-rate, or not an artist at all. To *this* rule there is no exception in any art.

—*Modern Painters*, Vol. III, "Of the True Ideal:—Secondly, Naturalist" (1856)

⋆

{"The general way in which the great men speak is of '*trying* to do' this or that"}

[. . .] every great composition is in perfect harmony with all true rules, and involves thousands too delicate for ear, or eye, or thought, to trace; still it is possible to reason, with infinite pleasure and profit, about these principles, when the thing is once done; only, all our reasoning will not enable any one to do another thing like it, because all reasoning falls infinitely short of the divine instinct. Thus we may reason wisely over the way a bee builds its comb, and be profited by finding out certain things about the angles of it. But the bee knows nothing about those matters. It builds its comb in a far more inevitable way. And, from a bee to Paul Veronese, all master-workers work with this awful, this inspired unconsciousness.

I said just now that there was no exception to *this* law, that the great men never knew how or why they did things. It is, of course, only with caution that such a broad statement should be made; but I have seen much of different kinds of artists, and I have always found the knowledge of, and attention to, rules so *accurately* in the inverse ratio to the power of the painter, that I have myself no doubt that the law is constant, and that men's smallness may be trigonometrically estimated by the attention which, in their work, they pay to principles, especially principles of composition. The general way in which the great men speak is of "*trying* to do" this or that, just as a child would tell of something he had seen and could not utter. Thus, in speaking of the drawing of which I have given an etching farther on (a scene on the St. Gothard), Turner asked if I had been to see "that litter of stones which I *endeavored* to represent;" and William Hunt, when I asked him one day as he was painting, why he put on such and such a colour, answered, "I don't know; I am just *aiming* at it;" and Turner, and he, and all the other men I have known who could paint, always spoke and speak in the same way; not in any selfish restraint of their knowledge, but in pure simplicity. While all the men whom I know, who *cannot* paint, are ready with admirable reasons for everything they have done; and can show, in the most conclusive way, that Turner is wrong, and how he might be improved.

—*Modern Painters*, Vol. III, "Of the True Ideal:—Secondly, Naturalist" (1856)

★

{"the greatest thing a human soul ever does in this world is to *see* something"}

Again: another very important, though not infallible, test of greatness is, as we have often said, the appearance of Ease with which the thing is done. It may be that, as with Dante and Leonardo, the finish given to the work effaces the evidence of ease; but where the ease is manifest, as in Scott, Turner, and Tintoret; and the thing done is very noble, it is a strong reason for placing the men above those who confessedly work with great pains. Scott writing his chapter or two before breakfast—not retouching, Turner finishing a whole drawing in a forenoon before he goes out to shoot (providing always the chapter and drawing be good), are instantly to be set above men who confessedly have spent the day over work, and think the hours well spent if it has been a little mended between sunrise and sunset. Indeed, it is no use for men to think to appear great by working fast, dashing, and scrawling; the thing they do must be good and great, cost what time it may; but if it *be* so, and they have honestly and unaffectedly done it with *no effort*, it is probably a greater and better thing than the result of the hardest efforts of others.

Then, as touching the kind of work done by these two men, the more I think of it I find this conclusion more impressed upon me,—that the greatest thing a human soul ever does in this world is to *see* something, and tell what it *saw* in a plain way. Hundreds of people can talk for one who can think, but thousands can think for one who can see. To see clearly is poetry, prophecy, and religion,—all in one.

—*Modern Painters*, Vol. III, "Of Modern Landscape" (1856)

★

{"what qualities chiefly distinguish great artists from feeble artists"}

If we were to be asked, abruptly, and required to answer briefly, what qualities chiefly distinguish great artists from feeble artists, we should answer, I suppose, first, their sensibility and tenderness; secondly, their imagination; and thirdly, their industry. Some of us might, perhaps, doubt the justice of attaching so much importance to this last character, because we have all known clever men who were indolent, and dull men who were industrious. But though you may have known clever men who were indolent, you never knew a *great* man who was so; and, during such investigation as I have been able to give to the lives of the artists whose works are in all points noblest, no fact ever looms so large upon me—no law remains so steadfast in the universality of its application, as the fact and law that they are all great workers: nothing concerning them is matter of more astonishment than the quantity they have accomplished in the given length of their life; and when I hear a young man spoken of, as giving promise of high genius, the first question I ask about him is always—

Does he work?

—*The Two Paths*, "Influence of Imagination in Architecture" (1858)

★

{"as the made thing is good or bad, so is the maker of it"}

The faults of a work of art are the faults of its workmen, and its virtues his virtues.

Great art is the expression of the mind of a great man, and mean art, that of the want of mind of a weak man. A foolish person builds foolishly, and a wise one, sensibly; a virtuous one, beautifully; and a vicious one, basely. If stone work is well put together, it means that a thoughtful man planned it, and a careful man cut it, and an honest man cemented it. If it has too much ornament, it means that its carver was too greedy of pleasure; if too little, that he was rude, or insensitive, or stupid, and the like. So that when once you have learned how to spell these precious of all legends,—pictures and buildings,—you may read the characters of men, and of nations, in their art, as in a mirror;—nay, as in a microscope, and magnified a hundredfold; for the character becomes passionate in the art, and intensifies itself in all its noblest or meanest delights. Nay, not only as in a microscope, but as under a scalpel, and in dissection; for a man may hide himself from you, or misrepresent himself to you, every other way; but he cannot in his work: there, be sure, you have him to the inmost. All that he likes, all that he sees,—all that he can do,—his imagination, his clumsiness, cleverness, everything is there. If the work is a cobweb, you know it was made by a spider; if a honeycomb, by a bee; a worm cast is thrown up by a worm, and a nest wreathed by a bird; and a house built by a man, worthily, if he is worthy, and ignobly, if he is ignoble.

And always, from the least to the greatest, as the made thing is good or bad, so is the maker of it.

[. . .] You will find in the end, that *no man could have done it but exactly the man who did it*; and by looking close at it, you may, if you know your letters, read precisely the manner of man he was.

—*The Queen of the Air*, "Athena Ergane" (1869)

⋆

{"the movement of the hand of a great painter is at every instant governed by a direct and new intention"}

[. . .] the day's work of a man like Mantegna or Paul Veronese consists of an unfaltering, uninterrupted succession of movements of the hand more precise than those of the finest fencer: the pencil leaving one point and arriving at another, not only with unerring precision at the extremity of the line, but with an unerring and yet varied course—sometimes over spaces a foot or more in extent—yet a course so determined everywhere, that either of these men could, and Veronese often does, draw a finished profile, or any other portion of the contour of the face, with one line, not afterwards changed. Try, first, to realise to yourselves the muscular precision of that action, and the intellectual strain of it; for the movement of a fencer is perfect in practised monotony; but the movement of the hand of a great painter is at every instant governed by a direct and new intention. Then imagine that muscular firmness and subtlety, and the instantaneously selective and ordinant energy of the brain, sustained all day long, not only without fatigue, but with a visible joy in the exertion, like that which an eagle seems to take in the wave of his wings; and this all life long, and through long life, not only without failure of power, but with visible increase of it, until the actually organic changes of old age. And then consider, so far as you know anything of physiology, what sort of an ethical state of body and mind that means! ethic through ages past! what fineness of race there must be to get it, what exquisite balance and symmetry of the vital powers! And then, finally, determine for yourselves whether a manhood like that is consistent with any viciousness of soul, with any mean anxiety, any gnawing lust, any wretchedness of spite or remorse, any consciousness of rebellion against law of God or man, or any actual, though unconscious violation of even the least law to which obedience is essential for the glory of life and the pleasing of its Giver.

—*Lectures on Art*, "The Relation of Art to Morals" (1870)

★

{"As long as you can see anything, you can see—almost all"}

It is the crowning virtue of all great art that, however little is left of it by the injuries of time, that little will be lovely. As long as you can see anything, you can see—almost all;—so much the hand of the master will suggest of his soul.

—*Mornings in Florence*, "The First Morning. Santa Croce" (1875–1877)

★

{". . . the greatest masters . . . never expect you to look at them"}

It is a characteristic—(as far as I know, quite a universal one)—of the greatest masters, that they never expect you to look at them; seem always rather surprised if you want to; and not overpleased. Tell them you are going to hang their picture at the upper end of the table at the next great City dinner, and that Mr. So and So will make a speech about it; you produce no impression upon them whatever, or an unfavourable one. The chances are ten to one they send you the most rubbishy thing they can find in their lumber-room. But send for one of them in a hurry, and tell him the rats have gnawed a nasty hole behind the parlor door, and you want it plastered and painted over;—and he does you a masterpiece which the world will peep behind your door to look at for ever.

I have no time to tell you why this is so; nor do I know why, altogether; but so it is.

—*Mornings in Florence*, "The Third Morning. Before the Soldan" (1875–1877)

Landscape Painting

{The artist "has only to ask himself whether he cares for anything except himself"}

[. . .] THIS IS THE chief fault of our English landscapists, that they have not the intense all-observing penetration of well-balanced mind; they have not, except in one or two instances, anything of that feeling which Wordsworth shows in the following lines:—

> So far, so sweet, withal so sensitive;—
> Would that the little flowers were born to live
> Conscious of half the pleasure which they give.
> That to this mountain daisy's self were known
> *The beauty of its star-shaded shadow thrown*
> *On the smooth surface of this naked stone.*

That is a little bit of good, downright, foreground painting—no mistake about it; daisy, and shadow, and stone, texture and all. Our painters must come to this before they have done their duty; and yet, on the other hand, let them beware of finishing, for the sake of finish, all over their picture. The ground is not to be all over daisies, nor is every daisy to have its star-shaped shadow; there is as much finish in the right concealment of things as in the right exhibition of them; and while I demand this amount of specific character where nature shows it, I demand equal fidelity to her where she conceals it. To paint mist rightly, space rightly, and light rightly, it may be often necessary to paint nothing else rightly, but the rule is simple for all that; if the artist is painting something that he knows and loves, as he knows it because he loves it, whether it be the fair strawberry of Cima, or the clear sky of Francia, or the blazing incomprehensible mist of Turner, he is all right; but the moment he does anything as he thinks it ought to be, because he does not care about it, he is all wrong. He has only to ask himself whether he cares for anything except himself; so far as he does he will make a good picture; so far as he thinks of himself a vile one.

—*Modern Painters*, Vol. I, "General Application of the Foregoing Principles" (1843)

★

{"the artist not only *places* the spectator, but *talks* to him; makes him a sharer in his own strong feelings and quick thoughts"}

It cannot but be evident from the above division of the ideas conveyable by art, that the landscape painter must always have two great and distinct ends; the first, to induce in the spectator's mind the faithful conception of any natural objects whatsoever; the second, to guide the spectator's mind to those objects most worthy of its contemplation, and to inform him of the thoughts and feelings with which these were regarded by the artist himself.

In attaining the first end, the painter only places the spectator where he stands himself; he sets him before the landscape and leaves him. The spectator is alone. He may follow out his own thoughts as he would in the natural solitude, or he may remain untouched, unreflecting and regardless, as his disposition may incline him. But he has nothing of thought given to him, no new ideas, no unknown feelings, forced on his attention or his heart. The artist is his conveyance, not his companion,—his horse, not his friend. But in attaining the second end, the artist not only *places* the spectator, but *talks* to him; makes him a sharer in his own strong feelings and quick thoughts; hurries him away in his own enthusiasm; guides him to all that is beautiful; snatches him from all that is base, and leaves him more than delighted,—ennobled and instructed, under the sense of having not only beheld a new scene, but of having held communion with a new mind, and having been endowed for a time with the keen perception and the impetuous emotion of a nobler and more penetrating intelligence.

—*Modern Painters*, Vol. 1, "Of Ideas of Truth in Their Connection with Those of Beauty and Relation" (1843)

★

{"nothing is so great a proof of real imagination and invention, as the appearance that nothing has been imagined or invented"}

Nothing is so great a sign of truth and beauty in mountain drawing as the appearance of individuality—nothing is so great a proof of real imagination and invention, as the appearance that nothing has been imagined or invented. We ought to feel of every inch of mountain, that it *must* have existence in reality, that if we had lived near the place we should have known every crag of it, and that there must be people to whom every crevice and shadow of the picture is fraught with recollections, and coloured with associations. The moment the artist can make us feel this—the moment he can make us think that *he* has done nothing, that nature has done all—that moment he becomes ennobled, he proves himself great. As long as we remember him, we cannot respect him. We honor him most when we most forget him. He becomes great when he becomes invisible.

—*Modern Painters*, Vol. I, "Of the Inferior Mountains" (1843)

★

{"It is at your own will that you see in that despised stream, either the refuse of the street, or the image of the sky"}

Now, the fact is, that there is hardly a roadside pond or pool which has not as much landscape *in* it as above it. It is not the brown, muddy, dull thing we suppose it to be; it has a heart like ourselves, and in the bottom of that there are the boughs of the tall trees, and the blades of the shaking grass, and all manner of hues, of variable, pleasant light out of the sky; nay, the ugly gutter, that stagnates over the drain bars, in the heart of the foul city, is not altogether base; down in that, if you will look deep enough, you may see the dark, serious blue of far-off sky, and the passing of pure clouds. It is at your own will that you see in that despised stream, either the refuse of the street, or the image of the sky—so it is with almost all other things that we unkindly despise. Now, this farseeing is just the difference between the great and the vulgar painter; the common man *knows* the roadside pool is muddy, and draws its mud; the great painter sees beneath and behind the brown surface what will take him a day's work to follow, but he follows it, cost what it will. And if painters would only go out to the nearest common and take the nearest dirty pond among the furze, and draw that thoroughly, not considering that it is water that they are drawing, and that water must be done in a certain way; but drawing determinedly what they *see*, that is to say, all the trees, and their shaking leaves, and all the hazy passages of disturbing sunshine; and the bottom seen in the clearer little bits at the edge, and the stones of it, and all the sky, and the clouds far down in the middle, drawn as completely, and more delicately than they must be, than the real clouds above, they would come home with such a notion of water-painting as might save me and every one else all trouble of writing more about the matter; but now they do nothing of the kind, but take the ugly, round, yellow surface for granted, or else improve it, and, instead of giving that refined, complex, delicate, but saddened and gloomy reflection in the polluted water, they clear it up with coarse flashes of yellow, and green, and blue, and spoil their own eyes, and hurt ours; failing, of course, still more hopelessly in touching the pure, inimitable light of waves thrown loose; and so Canaletto is still thought to have painted canals, and Vandevelde and Backhuysen to have painted sea, and the uninterpreted streams and maligned seas hiss shame upon us from their rocky beds and hollow shores.

—*Modern Painters*, Vol. I, "Of Water, as Painted by the Ancients" (1843)

★

{"Talkative facts are always more interesting and more important than silent ones"}

It ought farther to be observed respecting truths in general, that those are always most valuable which are most historical, that is, which tell us most about the past and future states of the object to which they belong. In a tree, for instance, it is more important to give the appearance of energy and elasticity in the limbs which is indicative of growth and life, than any particular character of leaf, or texture of bough. It is more important that we should feel that the uppermost sprays are creeping higher and higher into the sky, and be impressed with the current of life and motion which is animating every fibre, than that we should know the exact pitch of relief with which those fibres are thrown out against the sky. For the first truths tell us tales about the tree, about what it has been, and will be, while the last are characteristic of it only in its present state, and are in no way talkative about themselves. Talkative facts are always more interesting and more important than silent ones. So again the lines in a crag which mark its stratification, and how it has been washed and rounded by water, or twisted and drawn out in fire, are more important, because they tell more than the stains of the lichens which change year by year, and the accidental fissures of frost or decomposition; not but that both of these are historical, but historical in a less distinct manner, and for shorter periods.

Hence in general the truths of specific form are the first and most important of all; and next to them, those truths of chiaroscuro which are necessary to make us understand every quality and part of forms, and the relative distances of objects among each other, and in consequence their relative bulks. [. . .] To make us understand the *space* of the sky, is an end worthy of the artist's highest powers; to hit its particular blue or gold is an end to be thought of when we have accomplished the first, and not till then.

—*Modern Painters*, Vol. I, "Recapitulation" (1843)

*

{"Every attempt to produce that which shall be *any* rock, ends in the production of that which is *no* rock"}

[. . .] it will be the duty,—the imperative duty,—of the landscape painter, to descend to the lowest details with undiminished attention. Every herb and flower of the field has its specific, distinct, and perfect beauty; it has its peculiar habitation, expression, and function. The highest art is that which seizes this specific character, which develops and illustrates it, which assigns to it its proper position in the landscape, and which, by means of it, enhances and enforces the great impression which the picture is intended to convey. Nor is it of herbs and flowers alone that such scientific representation is required. Every class of rock, every kind of earth, every form of cloud, must be studied with equal industry, and rendered with equal precision. And thus we find ourselves unavoidably led to a conclusion directly opposed to that constantly enunciated dogma of the parrot-critic, that the features of nature must be "generalized,"—a dogma whose inherent and broad absurdity would long ago have been detected, if it had not contained in its convenient falsehood an apology for indolence, and a disguise for incapacity. Generalized! As if it were possible to generalize things generically different. [. . .]

An animal must be either one animal or another animal; it cannot be a general animal, or it is no animal; and so a rock must be either one rock or another rock; it cannot be a general rock, or it is no rock. If there were a creature in the foreground of a picture, of which he could not decide whether it were a pony or a pig, the Athenæum critic would perhaps affirm it to be a generalization of pony and pig, and consequently a high example of "harmonious union and simple effect." But *I* should call it simple bad drawing. And so when there are things in the foreground of Salvator of which I cannot pronounce whether they be granite or slate, or tufa, I affirm that there is in them neither harmonious union nor simple effect, but simple monstrosity. [. . .] We may, if we choose, put together centaur monsters; but they must still be half man, half horse; they cannot be both man and horse, nor either man or horse. And so, if landscape painters choose, they may give us rocks which shall be half granite and half slate; but they cannot give us rocks which shall be either granite or slate, nor which shall be both granite and slate. Every attempt to produce that which shall be *any* rock, ends in the production of that which is *no* rock.

—*Modern Painters*, Vol. I, "Preface to the Second Edition" (1843)

★

{"certain means and limitations being prescribed, only that *kind of truth* is to be expected which is consistent with those means"}

It was only towards the close of the thirteenth century that figure painting began to assume so perfect a condition as to require some elaborate suggestion of landscape background. Up to that time, if any natural object had to be represented, it was done in an entirely conventional way, as you see it upon Greek vases, or in a Chinese porcelain pattern; an independent tree or flower being set upon the white ground, or ground of any colour, wherever there was a vacant space for it, without the smallest attempt to imitate the real colours and relations of the earth and sky about it. But at the close of the thirteenth century, Giotto, and in the course of the fourteenth, Orcagna, sought, for the first time, to give some resemblance to nature in their backgrounds, and introduced behind their figures pieces of true landscape, formal enough still, but complete in intention, having foregrounds and distances, sky and water, forests and mountains, carefully delineated, not exactly in their true colour, but yet in colour approximating to the truth. The system which they introduced (for though in many points enriched above the work of earlier ages, the Orcagna and Giotto landscape was a very complete piece of recipe) was observed for a long period by their pupils, and may be thus briefly described:—The sky is always pure blue, paler at the horizon, and with a few streaky white clouds in it, the ground is green even to the extreme distance, with brown rocks projecting from it; water is blue streaked with white. The trees are nearly always composed of clusters of their proper leaves relieved on a black or dark ground [. . .]. And observe carefully, with respect to the complete drawing of the leaves on this tree, and the smallness of their number, the real distinction between noble conventionalism and false conventionalism.

You will often hear modern architects defending their monstrous ornamentation on the ground that it is "conventional," and that architectural ornament ought to be conventionalized. Remember, when you hear this, that noble conventionalism is not an agreement between the artist and spectator that the one shall misrepresent nature sixty times over, and the other believe the misrepresentation sixty times over, but it is an agreement that certain means and limitations being prescribed, only that *kind of truth* is to be expected which is consistent with those means. For instance, if Sir Joshua Reynolds had been talking to a friend about the character of a face, and there had been nothing in the room but a deal table and an inkbottle—and no pens—Sir Joshua would have dipped his finger in the ink, and painted a portrait on the table with his finger, and a noble portrait too; certainly not delicate in outline, nor representing any of the qualities of the face dependent on rich outline, but getting as much of the face as in that manner was attainable. That is noble conventionalism, and Egyptian work on granite, or illuminator's work in glass, is all conventional in the same sense, but not conventionally false. The two noblest and truest carved lions I have ever seen, are the two granite ones in the Egyptian room of the British Museum, and yet in them, the lions' manes and beards are represented by rings of solid rock, as smooth as a mirror!

[. . .] thus in Giotto's foliage, he *stops short* of the quantity of leaves on the real tree, but he gives you the form of the leaves represented with perfect truth. His foreground also is nearly always occupied by flowers and herbage, carefully and individually painted from nature; while, although thus simple in plan, the arrangements of line in these landscapes of course show the influence of the master-mind, and sometimes, where the story requires it, we find the usual formulæ overleaped, and Giotto at Avignon painting the breakers of the sea on a steep shore with great care, while Orcagna, in his Triumph of

Death, has painted a thicket of brambles mixed with teazles, in a manner worthy of the best days of landscape art.

—*Lectures on Architecture and Painting*, "Turner and His Works" (1853)

*

{"the calls upon the imagination are multiplied as a great painter finishes"}

[. . .] the truly great artist neither leaves the imagination to itself, like Sir Joshua, nor insults it by realization, like Hobbema, but finds it continual employment of the happiest kind. Having summoned it by his vigorous first touches, he says to it: "Here is a tree for you, and it is to be an oak. Now I know that you can make it green and intricate for yourself, but that is not enough: an oak is not only green and intricate, but its leaves have most beautiful and fantastic forms which I am very sure you are not quite able to complete without help; so I will draw a cluster or two perfectly for you, and then you can go on and do all the other clusters. So far so good: but the leaves are not enough; the oak is to be full of acorns, and you may not be quite able to imagine the way they grow, nor the pretty contrast of their glossy almond-shaped nuts with the chasing of their cups; so I will draw a bunch or two of acorns for you, and you can fill up the oak with others like them. Good: but that is not enough; it is to be a bright day in summer, and all the outside leaves are to be glittering in the sunshine as if their edges were of gold: I cannot paint this, but you can; so I will really gild some of the edges nearest you, and you can turn the gold into sunshine, and cover the tree with it. Well done: but still this is not enough; the tree is so full foliaged and so old that the wood birds come in crowds to build there; they are singing, two or three under the shadow of every bough. I cannot show you them all; but here is a large one on the outside spray, and you can fancy the others inside."

In this way the calls upon the imagination are multiplied as a great painter finishes; and from these larger incidents he may proceed into the most minute particulars, and lead the companion imagination to the veins in the leaves and the mosses on the trunk, and the shadows of the dead leaves upon the grass, but always multiplying thoughts, or subjects of thought, never working for the sake of realization; the amount of realization actually reached depending on his space, his materials, and the nature of the thoughts he wishes to suggest. In the sculpture of an oak tree, introduced above an Adoration of the Magi on the tomb of the Doge Marco Dolfino (fourteenth century), the sculptor has been content with a few leaves, a single acorn, and a bird; while, on the other hand, Millais' willow-tree with the robin, in the background of his *Ophelia*, or the foreground of Hunt's *Two Gentlemen of Verona*, carries the appeal to the imagination into particulars so multiplied and minute, that the work nearly reaches realization. But it does not matter how near realization the work may approach in its fulness, or how far off it may remain in its slightness, so long as realization is not the end proposed, but the informing one spirit of the thoughts of another. And in this greatness and simplicity of purpose all noble art is alike, however slight its means, or however perfect, from the rudest mosaics of St. Mark's to the most tender finishing of the *Huguenot* or the *Ophelia*.

—*The Stones of Venice*, Vol. III, "Conclusion" (1853)

★

{". . . all genius is useless, all labor is useless, if you do not give facts"}

There are some truths, easily obtained, which give a deceptive resemblance to Nature; others only to be obtained with difficulty, which cause no deception, but give inner and deep resemblance. These two classes of truths cannot be obtained together; choice must be made between them. The bad painter gives the cheap deceptive resemblance. The good painter gives the precious non-deceptive resemblance. Constable perceives in a landscape that the grass is wet, the meadows flat, and the boughs shady; that is to say, about as much as, I suppose, might in general be apprehended, between them, by an intelligent fawn and a skylark. Turner perceives at a glance the whole sum of visible truth open to human intelligence. So Berghem perceives nothing in a figure, beyond the flashes of light on the folds of its dress; but Michael Angelo perceives every flash of thought that is passing through its spirit; and Constable and Berghem may imitate windows; Turner and Michael Angelo can by no means imitate windows. But Turner and Michael Angelo are nevertheless the best.

"Well, but," the reader persists, "you admitted just now that because Turner did not get his work to look like a window there was something wrong in him."

I did so; if he were quite right he would have *all* truth, low as well as high; that is, he would be Nature and not Turner; but that is impossible to man. There is much that is wrong in him; much that is infinitely wrong in all human effort. But, nevertheless, in some an infinity of Betterness above other human effort.

"Well, but you said you would change your Turners for windows, why not, therefore, for Constables?"

Nay, I did not say that I would change them for windows *merely*, but for windows which commanded the chain of the Alps and Isola Bella. That is to say, for all the truth that there is in Turner, and all the truth besides which is not in him; but I would not change them for Constables, to have a small piece of truth which is not in Turner, and none of the mighty truth which there is.

Thus far, then, though the subject is one requiring somewhat lengthy explanation, it involves no real difficulty. There is not the slightest inconsistency in the mode in which throughout this work I have desired the relative merits of painters to be judged. I have always said, he who is closest to Nature is best. All rules are useless, all genius is useless, all labor is useless, if you do not give facts; the more facts you give the greater you are; and there is no fact so unimportant as to be prudently despised, if it be possible to represent it.

—*Modern Painters*, Vol. III, "Of the Use of Pictures" (1856)

★

{"the narrow spirit of correction could not cast itself fully into any scene"}

[. . .] a young German painter [. . .] had brought home a portfolio of sketches remarkable alike for their fidelity and purity. Every one was a laborious and accurate study of some particular spot. Every cottage, every cliff, every tree, at the site chosen, had been drawn; and drawn with palpable sincerity of portraiture, and yet in such a spirit that it was impossible to conceive that any sin or misery had ever entered into one of the scenes he had represented; and the volcanic horrors of Radicofani, the pestilent gloom of the Pontines, and the boundless despondency of the Campagna became under his hand, only various appearances of Paradise.

It was very interesting to observe the minute emendations or omissions by which this was effected. To set the tiles the slightest degree more in order upon a cottage roof; to insist upon the vine-leaves at the window, and let the shadow which fell from them naturally conceal the rent in the wall; to draw all the flowers in the foreground, and miss the weeds; to draw all the folds of the white clouds, and miss those of the black ones; to mark the graceful branches of the trees, and, in one way or another, beguile the eye from those which were ungainly; to give every peasant-girl whose face was visible the expression of an angel, and every one whose back was turned the bearing of a princess; finally, to give a general look of light, clear organization, and serene vitality to every feature in the landscape;—such were his artifices, and such his delights. It was impossible not to sympathize deeply with the spirit of such a painter; and it was just cause for gratitude to be permitted to travel, as it were, through Italy with such a friend. But his work had, nevertheless, its stern limitations and marks of everlasting inferiority. Always soothing and pathetic, it could never be sublime, never perfectly nor entrancingly beautiful; for the narrow spirit of correction could not cast itself fully into any scene; the calm cheerfulness which shrank from the shadow of the cypress, and the distortion of the olive, could not enter into the brightness of the sky that they pierced, nor the softness of the bloom that they bore: for every sorrow that his heart turned from, he lost a consolation; for every fear which he dared not confront, he lost a portion of his hardiness; the unsceptred sweep of the storm-clouds, the fair freedom of glancing shower and flickering sunbeam, sank into sweet rectitudes and decent formalisms; and, before eyes that refused to be dazzled or darkened, the hours of sunset wreathed their rays unheeded, and the mists of the Apennines spread their blue veils in vain.

—*Modern Painters*, Vol. III, "Of the True Ideal:—First, Purist" (1856)

*

{"if the mountain be lofty, and in light, it is so faint in colour that the eye literally cannot trace its separation from the hues next to it"}

Of all the various impossibilities which torment and humiliate the painter, none are more vexatious than that of drawing a mountain form. It is indeed impossible enough to draw, by resolute care, the foam on a wave, or the outline of the foliage of a large tree; but in these cases, when care is at fault, carelessness will help, and the dash of the brush will in some measure give wildness to the churning of the foam, and infinitude to the shaking of the leaves. But chance will not help us with the mountain. Its fine and faintly organized edge seems to be definitely traced against the sky; yet let us set ourselves honestly to follow it, and we find, on the instant, it has disappeared: and that for two reasons. The first, that if the mountain be lofty, and in light, it is so faint in colour that the eye literally cannot trace its separation from the hues next to it. The other day I wanted the contour of a limestone mountain in the Valais, distant about seven miles, and as many thousand feet above me; it was barren limestone; the morning sun fell upon it, so as to make it almost vermilion colour, and the sky behind it a bluish green. Two tints could hardly have been more opposed, but both were so subtle, that I found it impossible to see accurately the line that separated the vermilion from the green. The second, that if the contour be observed from a nearer point, or looked at when it is dark against the sky, it will be found composed of millions of minor angles, crags, points, and fissures, which no human sight or hand can draw finely enough, and yet all of which have effect upon the mind. [. . .]

And if not outlines, *a fortiori* not details of mass, which have all the complexity of the outline multiplied a thousand fold, and drawn in fainter colours. Nothing is more curious than the state of embarrassment into which the unfortunate artist must soon be cast when he endeavors honestly to draw the face of the simplest mountain cliff—say a thousand feet high, and two or three miles distant. It is full of exquisite details, all seemingly decisive and clear; but when he tries to arrest one of them, he cannot see it,—cannot find where it begins or ends,—and presently it runs into another; and then he tries to draw that, but that will not be drawn, neither, until it has conducted him to a third, which, somehow or another, made part of the first; presently he finds that, instead of three, there are in reality four, and then he loses his place altogether. He tries to draw clear lines, to make his work look craggy, but finds that then it is too hard; he tries to draw soft lines, and it is immediately too soft; he draws a curved line, and instantly sees it should have been straight; a straight one, and finds when he looks up again, that it has got curved while he was drawing it. There is nothing for him but despair, or some sort of abstraction and shorthand for cliff. Then the only question is, what is the wisest abstraction; and out of the multitude of lines that cannot altogether be interpreted, which are the really dominant ones; so that if we cannot give the whole, we may at least give what will convey the most important facts about the cliff.[21]

—*Modern Painters*, Vol. IV, "Resulting Forms:—First, Aiguilles" (1856)

★

{"We never see anything clearly"}

John Bellini, Leonardo, Angelico, Dürer, Perugino, Raphael,—all of them hated fog, and repudiated indignantly all manner of concealment. Clear, calm, placid, perpetual vision, far and near; endless perspicuity of space; unfatigued veracity of eternal light; perfectly accurate delineation of every leaf on the trees, every flower in the fields, every golden thread in the dresses of the figures, up to the highest point of calm brilliancy which was penetrable to the eye, or possible to the pencil,—these were their glory. On the other—the entirely mysterious—side, we have only sullen and sombre Rembrandt; desperate Salvator; filmy, futile Claude; occasionally some countenance from Correggio and Titian, and a careless condescension or two from Tintoret,—not by any means a balanced weight of authority. Then, even in modern times, putting Turner (who is at present the prisoner at the bar) out of the question, we have, in landscape, Stanfield and Harding as definers, against Copley Fielding and Robson on the side of the clouds; Mulready and Wilkie against Etty,—even Etty being not so much misty in conception as vague in execution, and not, therefore, quite legitimately to be claimed on the foggy side; while, finally, the whole body of the Pre-Raphaelites—certainly the greatest men, taken as a class, whom modern Europe has produced in concernment with the arts—entirely agree with the elder religious painters, and do, to their utmost, dwell in an element of light and declaration, in antagonism to all mist and deception. Truly, the clouds seem to be getting much the worst of it; and I feel, for the moment, as if nothing could be said for them. However, having been myself long a cloud-worshipper, and passed many hours of life in the pursuit of them from crag to crag, I must consider what can possibly be submitted in their defence, and in Turner's.

The first and principal thing to be submitted is, that the clouds *are there*. Whether we like them or not, it is a fact that by far the largest

[21] John Ruskin, *The Pass of Faido*, 1845, drawing.

spaces of the habitable world are full of them. That is Nature's will in the matter; and whatever we may theoretically determine to be expedient or beautiful, she has long ago determined what shall *be*. We may declare that clear horizons and blue skies form the most exalted scenery; but for all that, the bed of the river in the morning will still be traced by its line of white mist, and the mountain peaks will be seen at evening only in the rents between their blue fragments of towering cloud. Thus it is, and that so constantly, that it is impossible to become a faithful landscape painter without continually getting involved in effects of this kind. We may, indeed, avoid them systematically, but shall become narrow mannerists if we do.

But not only is there a *partial* and variable mystery thus caused by clouds and vapors throughout great spaces of landscape; there is a continual mystery caused throughout *all* spaces, caused by the absolute infinity of things. We never see anything clearly. [. . .] the fact is, that everything we look at, be it large or small, near or distant, has an equal quantity of mystery in it; and the only question is, not how much mystery there is, but at what part of the object mystification begins. We suppose we see the ground under our feet clearly, but if we try to number its grains of dust, we shall find that it is as full of confusion and doubtful form as anything else; so that there is literally *no* point of clear sight, and there never can be. What we call seeing a thing clearly, is only seeing enough of it to *make out what it is*; this point of intelligibility varying in distance for different magnitudes and kinds of things, while the appointed quantity of mystery remains nearly the same for all. Thus: throwing an open book and an embroidered handkerchief on a lawn, at a distance of half a mile we cannot tell which is which; that is the point of mystery for the whole of those things. They are then merely white spots of indistinct shape. We approach them, and perceive that one is a book, the other a handkerchief, but cannot read the one, nor trace the embroidery of the other. The mystery has ceased to be in the whole things, and has gone into their details. We go nearer, and can now read the text and trace the embroidery, but cannot see the fibres of the paper, nor the threads of the stuff. The mystery has gone into a third place. We take both up and look closely at them; we see the watermark and the threads, but not the hills and dales in the paper's surface, nor the fine fibres which shoot off from every thread. The mystery has gone into a fourth place, where it must stay, till we take a microscope, which will send it into a fifth, sixth, hundredth, or thousandth place, according to the power we use. When, therefore, we say, we see the book *clearly*, we mean only that we know it is a book. When we say that we see the letters clearly, we mean that we know what letters they are; and artists feel that they are drawing objects at a convenient distance when they are so near them as to know, and to be able in painting to show that they know, what the objects are, in a tolerably complete manner; but this power does not depend on any definite distance of the object, but on its size, kind, and distance, together; so that a small thing in the foreground may be precisely in the same *phase* or place of mystery as a large thing far away.

The other day, as I was lying down to rest on the side of the hill round which the Rhone sweeps in its main angle, opposite Martigny, and looking carefully across the valley to the ridge of the hill which rises above Martigny itself, then distant about four miles, a plantain seed-vessel about an inch long, and a withered head of a scabious half an inch broad, happened to be seen rising up, out of the grass near me, across the outline of the distant hill, so as seemingly to set themselves closely beside the large pines and chestnuts which fringed that distant ridge. The plantain was eight yards from me, and the scabious seven; and to my sight, at these distances, the plantain and the far away pines were equally clear (it being a clear day, and the sun stooping to the west). The pines, four miles off, showed their branches, but I could not count them; and two or three young and old Spanish chestnuts beside them showed their broken masses distinctly; but I could not count those masses, only I knew the trees to be chestnuts by their general look. The plantain and scabious in like manner I knew to be a plantain and scabious by their general look. I saw the plantain seed-vessel to be, somehow, rough, and that there were two little projections at the bottom of the scabious head which I knew to mean the leaves of the calyx; but I could no more count distinctly the seeds of the plantain, or the group of leaves forming the calyx of the scabious, than I could count the branches of the far-away pines.

Under these circumstances, it is quite evident that neither the pine nor plantain could have been rightly represented by a single dot or stroke of colour. Still less could they be represented by a definite drawing, on a small scale, of a pine with all its branches clear, or of a plantain with all its seeds clear. The round dot or long stroke would represent nothing, and the clear delineation too much. They were not mere dots of colour which I saw on the hill, but something full of essence of pine; out of which I could gather which were young and which were old, and discern the distorted and crabbed pines from the symmetrical and healthy pines; and feel how the evening sun was sending its searching threads among their dark leaves;—assuredly they were more than dots of colour. And yet not one of their boughs or outlines could be distinctly made out, or distinctly drawn. Therefore, if I had drawn either a definite pine, or a dot, I should have been equally wrong, the right lying in an inexplicable, almost inimitable, confusion between the two.

—*Modern Painters*, Vol. IV, "Of Turnerian Mystery:—
First, As Essential" (1856)

*

{"we have to show the individual character and liberty of the separate leaves"}

[. . .] it is in the perfect acknowledgment and expression of these *three* laws that all good drawing of landscape consists. There is, first, the organic unity; the law, whether of radiation, or parallelism, or concurrent action, which rules the masses of herbs and trees, of rocks, and clouds, and waves; secondly, the individual liberty of the members subjected to these laws of unity; and, lastly, the mystery under which the separate character of each is more or less concealed.

I say, first, there must be observance of the ruling organic law. This is the first distinction between good artists and bad artists. Your common sketcher or bad painter puts his leaves on the trees as if they were moss tied to sticks; he cannot see the lines of action or growth; he scatters the shapeless clouds over his sky, not perceiving the sweeps of associated curves which the real clouds are following as they fly; and he breaks his mountain side into rugged fragments, wholly unconscious of the lines of force with which the real rocks have risen, or of the lines of couch in which they repose. On the contrary, it is the main delight of the great draughtsman to trace these laws of government; and his tendency to error is always in the exaggeration of their authority rather than in its denial.

Secondly, I say, we have to show the individual character and liberty of the separate leaves, clouds, or rocks. And herein the great masters separate themselves finally from the inferior ones; for if the men of inferior genius ever express law at all, it is by the sacrifice of individuality. Thus, Salvator Rosa has great perception of the sweep of foliage and rolling of clouds, but never draws a single leaflet or mist wreath accurately. Similarly, Gainsborough, in his landscape, has great feeling for masses of form and harmony of colour; but in the detail gives nothing but meaningless touches; not even so much as the species of tree, much less the variety of its leafage, being ever discernible. Now, although both these expressions of government and individuality are essential to masterly work, the individuality is the *more* essential, and the more difficult of attainment; and, therefore, that attainment separates the great masters *finally* from the inferior ones.

—*The Elements of Drawing*, "Sketching from Nature" (1857)

★

{"If you can paint *one* leaf, you can paint the world"}

When, some few years ago, the pre-Raphaelites began to lead our wandering artists back into the eternal paths of all great Art, and showed that whatever men drew at all, ought to be drawn accurately and knowingly; not blunderingly nor by guess (leaves of trees among other things): as ignorant pride on the one hand refused their teaching, ignorant hope caught at it on the other. "What!" said many a feeble young student to himself. "Painting is not a matter of science then, nor or supreme skill, nor of inventive brain. I have only to go and paint the leaves of the trees as they grow, and I shall produce beautiful landscapes directly."

Alas! my innocent young friend. "Paint the leaves as they grow!" If you can paint *one* leaf, you can paint the world. These pre-Raphaelite laws, which you think so light, lay stern on the strength of Apelles and Zeuxis; put Titian to thoughtful trouble; are unrelaxed yet, and unrelaxable for ever. Paint a leaf indeed! Above-named Titian has done it: Correggio, moreover, and Giorgione: and Leonardo, very nearly, trying hard. Holbein, three or four times, in precious pieces, highest wrought. Raphael, it may be, on one or two crowns of Muse or Sibyl. If any one else, in later times, we have to consider.

—*Modern Painters*, Vol. V, "Leaf Aspects" (1860)

Lessons and Laws

{"the weakest among us has a gift, however seemingly trivial, which is peculiar to him"}

THAT THEN WHICH I would have the reader inquire respecting every work of art of undetermined merit submitted to his judgment, is not whether it be a work of especial grandeur, importance, or power; but whether it have *any* virtue or substance as a link in this chain of truth, whether it have recorded or interpreted anything before unknown, whether it have added one single stone to our heaven-pointing pyramid, cut away one dark bough, or leveled one rugged hillock in our path. This, if it be an honest work of art, it must have done, for no man ever yet worked honestly without giving some such help to his race. God appoints to every one of his creatures a separate mission, and if they discharge it honorably, if they quit themselves like men and faithfully follow that light which is in them, withdrawing from it all cold and quenching influence, there will assuredly come of it such burning as, in its appointed mode and measure, shall shine before men, and be of service constant and holy. Degrees infinite of lustre there must always be, but the weakest among us has a gift, however seemingly trivial, which is peculiar to him, and which worthily used will be a gift also to his race forever [. . .].

—*Modern Painters*, Vol. I, "General Application of the Foregoing Principles" (1843)

*

{"He draws nothing well who thirsts not to draw *every*thing"}

[. . .] the complaint so often made by young artists that they have not within their reach materials, or subjects enough for their fancy, is utterly groundless, and the sign only of their own blindness and inefficiency; for there is that to be seen in every street and lane of every city, that to be felt and found in every human heart and countenance, that to be loved in every road-side weed and moss-grown wall, which in the hands of faithful men, may convey emotions of glory and sublimity continual and exalted.

Let therefore the young artist beware of the spirit of choice, it is an insolent spirit at the best and commonly a base and blind one too, checking all progress and blasting all power, encouraging weaknesses, pampering partialities, and teaching us to look to accidents of nature for the help and the joy which should come from our own hearts. He draws nothing well who thirsts not to draw *every*thing; when a good painter shrinks, it is because he is humbled, not fastidious, when he stops, it is because he is surfeited, and not because he thinks nature has given him unkindly food, or that he fears famine. I have seen a man of true taste pause for a quarter of an hour to look at the channellings that recent rain had traced in a heap of cinders.

—*Modern Painters*, Vol. II, "Of Accuracy and Inaccuracy in Impressions of Sense" (1846)

★

{"A man who has the gift, will take up any style that is going"}

Originality of expression does not depend on invention of new words; nor originality in poetry on invention of new measures; nor, in painting, on invention of new colours, or new modes of using them. The chords of music, the harmonies of colour, the general principles of the arrangement of sculptural masses, have been determined long ago, and, in all probability, cannot be added to any more than they can be altered. Granting that they may be, such additions or alterations are much more the work of time and of multitudes than of individual inventors. We may have one Van Eyck, who will be known as the introducer of a new style once in ten centuries, but he himself will trace his invention to some accidental bye-play or pursuit; and the use of that invention will depend altogether on the popular necessities or instincts of the period. Originality depends on nothing of the kind. A man who has the gift, will take up any style that is going, the style of his day, and will work in that, and be great in that, and make everything that he does in it look as fresh as if every thought of it had just come down from heaven. I do not say that he will not take liberties with his materials or with his rules: I do not say that strange changes will not sometimes be wrought by his efforts, or his fancies, in both. But those changes will be instructive, natural, facile, though sometimes marvelous; they will never be sought after as things necessary to his dignity or to his independence; and those liberties will be like the liberties that a great speaker takes with the language, not a defiance of its rules for the sake of singularity; but inevitable, uncalculated, and brilliant consequences of an effort to express what the language, without such infraction, could not. [. . .]

Neither originality, therefore, nor change, good though both may be, and this is commonly a most merciful and enthusiastic supposition with respect to either, are ever to be sought in themselves, or can ever be healthily obtained by any struggle or rebellion against common laws. We want neither the one nor the other. The forms of architecture already known are good enough for us, and for far better than any of us: and it will be time enough to think of changing them for better when we can use them as they are.

—*The Seven Lamps of Architecture*, "The Lamp of Life" (1849)

⋆

{"if a great thing can be done at all, it can be done easily"}

Let this single fact be quietly meditated upon by our ordinary painters, and they will see the truth of what was above asserted,—that if a great thing can be done at all, it can be done easily; and let them not torment themselves with twisting of compositions this way and that, and repeating, and experimenting, and scene-shifting. If a man can compose at all, he can compose at once, or rather he must compose in spite of himself. And this is the reason of that silence which I have kept in most of my works, on the subject of Composition. Many critics, especially the architects, have found fault with me for not "teaching people how to arrange masses;" for not "attributing sufficient importance to composition." Alas! I attribute far more importance to it than they do;—so much importance, that I should just as soon think of sitting down to teach a man how to write a *Divina Commedia*, or *King Lear*, as how to "compose," in the true sense, a single building or picture. The marvellous stupidity of this age of lecturers is, that they do not see that what they call "principles of composition," are mere principles of common sense in everything, as well as in pictures and buildings;—A picture is to have a principal light? Yes; and so a dinner is to have a principal dish, and an oration a principal point, and an air of music a principal note, and every man a principal object. A picture is to have harmony of relation among its parts? Yes; and so is a speech well uttered, and an action well ordered, and a company well chosen, and a ragout well mixed. Composition! As if a man were not composing every moment of his life, well or ill, and would not do it instinctively in his picture as well as elsewhere, if he could.

Composition of this lower or common kind is of exactly the same importance in a picture that it is in any thing else,—no more. It is well that a man should say what he has to say in good order and sequence, but the main thing is to say it truly. And yet we go on preaching to our pupils as if to have a principal light was every thing, and so cover our academy walls with Shacabac feasts, wherein the courses are indeed well ordered, but the dishes empty.

—*Pre-Raphaelitism* (1851)

★

{"one does not improve either violet or grass in gathering it, but one makes the flower visible"}

Is there, then, nothing to be done by man's art? Have we only to copy, and again copy, for ever, the imagery of the universe? Not so. We have work to do upon it; there is not any one of us so simple, nor so feeble, but he has work to do upon it. But the work is not to improve, but to explain. This infinite universe is unfathomable, inconceivable, in its whole; every human creature must slowly spell out, and long contemplate, such part of it as may be possible for him to reach; then set forth what he has learned of it for those beneath him; extricating it from infinity, as one gathers a violet out of grass; one does not improve either violet or grass in gathering it, but one makes the flower visible; and then the human being has to make its power upon his own heart visible also, and to give it the honor of the good thoughts it has raised up in him, and to write upon it the history of his own soul.

—*The Stones of Venice*, Vol. I, "The Vestibule" (1851)

★

{"the clever child [. . .] finds other means of expressing himself with his pencil"}

Suppose you have to teach two children drawing, one thoroughly clever and active-minded, the other dull and slow; and you put before them Julien's chalk studies of heads—*etudes a deux crayons*—and desire them to be copied. The dull child will slowly do your bidding, blacken his paper and rub it white again, and patiently and painfully, in the course of three or four years, attain to the performance of a chalk head, not much worse than his original, but still of less value than the paper it is drawn upon. But the clever child will not, or will only by force, consent to this discipline. He finds other means of expressing himself with his pencil somehow or another; and presently you find his paper covered with sketches of his grandfather and grandmother, and uncles and cousins,—sketches of the room, and the house, and the cat, and the dog, and the country outside, and everything in the world he can set his eyes on; and he gets on, and even his child's works has a value in it—a truth which makes it worth keeping; no one knows how precious, perhaps, that portrait of his grandfather may be, if any one has but the sense to keep it till the time when the old man can be seen no more up the lawn, nor by the wood.

—*Lectures on Architecture and Painting*, "Pre-Raphaelitism" (1853)

*

{"the entire method and aim of our art-teaching [. . .] destroys the greater number of its pupils altogether"}

[. . .] the wonderful thing is, that of all these men whom you now have come to call the great masters, there was *not one* who confessedly did not paint his own present world, plainly and truly. Homer sang of what he saw; Phidias carved what he saw; Raphael painted the men of his own time in their own caps and mantles; and every man who has arisen to eminence in modern times has done so altogether by his working in their way, and doing the things he saw. How did Reynolds rise? Not by painting Greek women, but by painting the glorious little living Ladies this, and Ladies that, of his own time. How did Hogarth rise? Not by painting Athenian follies, but London follies. Who are the men who have made an impression upon you yourselves—upon your own age? I suppose the most popular painter of the day is Landseer. Do you suppose he studied dogs and eagles out of the Elgin Marbles? And yet in the very face of these plain, incontrovertible, all-visible facts, we go on from year to year with the base system of Academy teaching, in spite of which every one of these men has risen: I say *in spite* of the entire method and aim of our art-teaching. It destroys the greater number of its pupils altogether; it hinders and paralyzes the greatest. There is not a living painter whose eminence is not in spite of everything he has been taught from his youth upwards, and who, whatever his eminence may be, has not suffered much injury in the course of his victory. For observe: this love of what is called ideality or beauty in preference to truth, operates not only in making us choose the past rather than the present for our subjects, but it makes us falsify the present when we do take it for our subject. I said just now that portrait-painters were historical painters;—so they are; but not good ones, because not faithful ones.[22]

The beginning and end of modern portraiture is adulation. The painters cannot live but by flattery; we should desert them if they spoke honestly. And therefore we can have no good portraiture; for in the striving after that which is *not* in their model, they lose the inner and deeper nobleness which *is* in their model. I saw not long ago, for the first time, the portrait of a man whom I knew well—a young man, but a religious man—and one who had suffered much from sickness. The whole dignity of his features and person depended upon the expression of serene, yet solemn, purpose sustaining a feeble frame; and the painter, by way of flattering him, strengthened him, and made him athletic in body, gay in countenance, idle in gesture; and the whole power and being of the man himself were lost.

—*Lectures on Architecture and Painting*, "Pre-Raphaelitism" (1853)

★

{"all good art has the *capacity of pleasing*"}

All things that are worth doing in art, are interesting and attractive when they are done. There is no law of right which consecrates dullness. The proof of a thing's being right is, that it has power over the heart; that it excites us, wins us, or helps us. I do not say that it has influence over all, but it has over a large class, one kind of art being fit for one class, and another for another; and there is no

[22] Joshua Reynolds, *Sir Watkin Williams-Wynn and his Mother*, c. 1768–9, painting.

goodness in art which is independent of the power of pleasing. Yet, do not mistake me; I do not mean that there is no such thing as neglect of the best art, or delight in the worst, just as many men neglect nature, and feed upon what is artificial and base; but I mean, that all good art has the *capacity of pleasing*, if people will attend to it; that there is no law against its pleasing; but, on the contrary, something wrong either in the spectator or the art, when it ceases to please. Now, therefore, if you feel that your present school of architecture is unattractive to you, I say there is something wrong, either in the architecture or in you; and I trust you will not think I mean to flatter you when I tell you, that the wrong is *not* in you, but in the architecture.

—*Lectures on Architecture and Painting*, "Architecture" (1853)

★

{"the true artist has that inspiration in him which is above all law"}

[. . .] all written or writable law respecting the arts is for the childish and ignorant: that in the beginning of teaching, it is possible to say that this or that must or must not be done; and laws of colour and shade may be taught, as laws of harmony are to the young scholar in music. But the moment a man begins to be anything deserving the name of an artist, all this teachable law has become a matter of course with him; and if, thenceforth, he boast himself anywise in the law, or pretend that he lives and works by it, it is a sure sign that he is merely tithing cumin,[23] and that there is no true art nor religion in him. For the true artist has that inspiration in him which is above all law, or rather, which is continually working out such magnificent and perfect obedience to supreme law, as can in no wise be rendered by line and rule. There are more laws perceived and fulfilled in the single stroke of a great workman, than could be written in a volume. His science is inexpressibly subtle, directing taught him by his Maker, not in any wise communicable or imitable. Neither can any written or definitely observable laws enable us to do any great thing. It is possible, by measuring and administering quantities of colour, to paint a room wall so that it shall not hurt the eye; but there are no laws by observing which we can become Titians. It is possible so to measure and

[23] This biblical expression, "tithing cumin," means paying attention to minor details at the expense of important ones.

administer syllables, as to construct harmonious verse; but there are no laws by which we can write *Iliads*. Out of the poem or the picture, once produced, men may elicit laws by the volume, and study them with advantage, to the better understanding of the existing poem or picture; but no more write or paint another, than by discovering laws of vegetation they can make a tree to grow. And therefore, wheresoever we find the system and formality of rules much dwelt upon, and spoken of as anything else than a help for children, there we may be sure that noble art is not even understood, far less reached. And thus it was with all the common and public mind in the fifteenth and sixteenth centuries. The greater men, indeed, broke through the thorn hedges; and, though much time was lost by the learned among them in writing Latin verses and anagrams, and arranging the framework of quaint sonnets and dexterous syllogisms, still they tore their way through the sapless thicket by force of intellect or of piety; for it was not possible that, either in literature or in painting, rules could be received by any strong mind, so as materially to interfere with its originality: and the crabbed discipline and exact scholarship became an advantage to the men who could pass through and despise them; so that in spite of the rules of the drama we had Shakespeare, and in spite of the rules of art we had Tintoret,—both of them, to this day, doing perpetual violence to the vulgar scholarship and dim-eyed proprieties of the multitude.[24]

—*The Stones of Venice*, Vol. III, "Roman Renaissance" (1853)

★

{"knowledge is not only very often unnecessary, but it is often *untrustworthy*"}

Nothing can be done well in art, except by vision. Scientific principles and experiences are helps to the eye, as a microscope is; and they are of exactly as much use *without* the eye. No science of perspective, or of anything else, will enable us to draw the simplest natural line accurately, unless we see it and feel it. Science is soon at her wits' end. All the professors of perspective in Europe, could not, by perspective, draw the line of curve of a sea beach; nay, could not outline one pool of the quiet water left among the sand. The eye

[24] Jacopo Tintoretto, *Judith and Holofernes*, 1577, painting.

and hand can do it, nothing else. All the rules of aerial perspective that ever were written, will not tell me how sharply the pines on the hill-top are drawn at this moment on the sky. I shall know if I see them, and love them; not till then. I may study the laws of atmospheric gradation for fourscore years and ten, and I shall not be able to draw so much as a brick-kiln through its own smoke, unless I look at it; and that in an entirely humble and unscientific manner, ready to see all that the smoke, my master, is ready to show me, and expecting to see nothing more.

So that all the knowledge a man has must be held cheap, and neither trusted nor respected, the moment he comes face to face with Nature. If it help him, well; if not, but, on the contrary, thrust itself upon him in an impertinent and contradictory temper, and venture to set itself in the slightest degree in opposition to, or comparison with, his sight, let it be disgraced forthwith. [. . .]

And observe, also, knowledge is not only very often unnecessary, but it is often *untrustworthy*. It is inaccurate, and betrays us where the eye would have been true to us. Let us take the single instance of the knowledge of aerial perspective, of which the moderns are so proud, and see how it betrays us in various ways. First by the conceit of it, which often prevents our enjoying work in which higher and better things were thought of than effects of mist. The other day I showed a line impression of Albert Dürer's "St. Hubert" to a modern engraver, who had never seen it nor any other of Albert Dürer's works.[25] He looked at it for a minute contemptuously, then turned away: "Ah, I see that man did not know much about aerial perspective!" All the glorious work and thought of the mighty master, all the redundant landscape, the living vegetation, the magnificent truth of line, were dead letters to him, because he happened to have been taught one particular piece of knowledge which Dürer despised.

—*The Stones of Venice*, Vol. III, "The Immeasurable, Intangible, and Indivisible" (1853)

★

{"Great art is precisely that which never was, nor will be taught"}

[. . .] every system of teaching is false which holds forth "great art" as in any wise to be taught to students, or even to be aimed at by them. Great art is precisely that which never was, nor will be taught,

[25] Albert Dürer, *St. Eustace*, c. 1501, engraving.

it is pre-eminently and finally the expression of the spirits of great men; so that the only wholesome teaching is that which simply endeavors to fix those characters of nobleness in the pupil's mind, of which it seems easily susceptible; and without holding out to him, as a possible or even probable result, that he should ever paint like Titian, or carve like Michael Angelo, enforces upon him the manifest possibility, and assured duty, of endeavoring to draw in a manner at least honest and intelligible; and cultivates in him those general charities of heart, sincerities of thought, and graces of habit which are likely to lead him, throughout life, to prefer openness to affectation, realities to shadows, and beauty to corruption.

—*Modern Painters*, Vol. III, "Of the Real Nature of Greatness of Style" (1856)

★

{"all that we call ideal in Greek or any other art [. . .] was, to the makers of it, true and existent"}

[. . .] the whole power, whether of painter or poet, to describe rightly what we call an ideal thing, depends upon its being thus, to him, not an ideal, but a *real* thing. No man ever did or ever will work well, but either from actual sight or sight of faith; and all that we call ideal in Greek or any other art, because to us it is false and visionary was, to the makers of it, true and existent. The heroes of Phidias are simply representations of such noble human persons as he every day saw, and the gods of Phidias simply representations of such noble divine persons as he thoroughly believed to exist, and did in mental vision truly behold. Hence I said in the second preface to *The Seven Lamps of Architecture*: "All great art represents something that it sees or believes in; nothing unseen or uncredited."

And just because it is always something that it sees or believes in, there is the peculiar character above noted, almost unmistakable, in all high and true ideas, of having been as it were studied from the life, and involving pieces of sudden familiarity, and close *specific* painting which never would have been admitted or even thought of, had not the painter drawn either from the bodily life or from the life of faith. For instance, Dante's centaur, Chiron, dividing his beard with his arrow before he can speak, is a thing that no mortal would ever have thought of, if he had not actually seen the centaur do it. They might have composed handsome bodies of men and horses in all possible ways, through a whole life of pseudo-idealism, and yet never dreamed of any such thing. But the real living centaur actually trotted across Dante's brain, and he saw him do it.

—*Modern Painters*, Vol. III, "Of the True Ideal:—
Secondly, Naturalist" (1856)

★

{"Is it so?"}

[. . .] so much grievous difficulty stands in the way of obtaining *real opinion* about pictures at all. Tell any man, of the slightest imaginative power, that such and such a picture is good, and means this or that: tell him, for instance, that a Claude is good, and that it means trees, and grass, and water; and forthwith, whatever faith, virtue, humility, and imagination there are in the man, rise up to help Claude, and to declare that indeed it is all "excellent good, i'faith;" and whatever in the course of his life he has felt of pleasure in trees and grass, he will begin to reflect upon and enjoy anew, supposing all the while it is the picture he is enjoying. Hence, when once a painter's reputation is accredited, it must be a stubborn kind of person indeed whom he will not please, or seem to please; for all the vain and weak people pretend to be pleased with him, for their own credit's sake, and all the humble and imaginative people seriously and honestly fancy they *are* pleased with him, deriving indeed, very certainly, delight from his work, but a delight which, if they were kept in the same temper, they would equally derive (and, indeed, constantly do derive) from the grossest daub that can be manufactured in imitation by the pawnbroker. Is, therefore, the pawnbroker's imitation as good as the original? Not so. There is the certain test of goodness and badness, which I am always striving to get people to use. As long as they are satisfied if they find their feelings pleasantly stirred and their fancy gaily occupied, so long there is for them no good, no bad. Anything may please, or anything displease, them; and their entire manner of thought and talking about art is mockery, and all their judgments are laborious injustices. But let them, in the teeth of their pleasure or displeasure, simply put the calm question,—Is it so? Is that the way a stone is shaped, the way a cloud is wreathed, the way a leaf is veined? and they are safe. They will do no more injustice to themselves nor to other men; they will learn to whose guidance they may trust their imagination, and from whom they must for ever withhold its reins.

"Well, but why have you dragged in this poor spectator's imagination at all, if you have nothing more to say for it than this; if you are merely going to abuse it, and go back to your tiresome facts?"

Nay; I am not going to abuse it. On the contrary, I have to assert, in a temper profoundly venerant of it, that though we must not suppose everything is right when this is aroused, we may be sure that something is wrong when this is *not* aroused. The something wrong may be in the spectator or in the picture; and if the picture be demonstrably in accordance with truth, the odds are, that it is in the spectator; but there is wrong somewhere; for the work of the picture is indeed eminently to get at this imaginative power in the beholder, and all its facts are of no use whatever if it does not. No matter how much truth it tells if the hearer be asleep. Its first work is to wake him, then to teach him.

—*Modern Painters*, Vol. III, "Of the Use of Pictures" (1856)

*

{"you will soon begin to understand under what a universal law of obscurity we live"}

Take the commonest, closest, most familiar thing, and strive to draw it verily as you see it. Be sure of this last fact, for otherwise you will find yourself continually drawing, not what you *see*, but what you *know*. The best practice to begin with is, sitting about three yards, from a bookcase (not your own, so that you may *know* none of the titles of the books), to try to draw the books accurately, with the titles on the backs, and patterns on the bindings, as you see them. You are not to stir from your place to look what they are, but to draw them simply as they appear, giving the perfect look of neat lettering; which, nevertheless, must be (as you find it on most of the books) absolutely illegible. Next try to draw a piece of patterned muslin or lace (of which you do not know the pattern), a little way off, and rather in the shade; and be sure you get all the grace and *look* of the pattern without going a step nearer to see what it is. Then try to draw a bank of grass, with all its blades; or a bush, with all its leaves; and you will soon begin to understand under what a universal law of obscurity we live, and perceive that all *distinct* drawing must be *bad* drawing, and that nothing can be right, till it is unintelligible.

—*Modern Painters*, Vol. IV, "Of Turnerian Mystery:—First, As Essential" (1856)

★

{"I do not think it advisable to engage a child in any but the most voluntary practice of art"}

I do not think it advisable to engage a child in any but the most voluntary practice of art. If it has talent for drawing, it will be continually scrawling on what paper it can get; and should be allowed to scrawl at its own free will, due praise being given for every appearance of care, or truth, in its efforts. It should be allowed to amuse itself with cheap colours almost as soon as it has sense enough to wish for them. If it merely daubs the paper with shapeless stains, the colour-box may be taken away till it knows better: but as soon as it begins painting red coats on soldiers, striped flags to ships, etc., it should have colours at command; and, without restraining its choice of subject in that imaginative and historical art, of a military tendency, which children delight in, (generally quite as valuable, by the way, as any historical art delighted in by their elders,) it should be gently led by the parents to try to draw, in such childish fashion as may be, the things it can see and likes,—birds, or butterflies, or flowers, or fruit.

In later years, the indulgence of using the colour should only be granted as a reward, after it has shown care and progress in its drawings with pencil.

—*The Elements of Drawing*, Preface (1857)

★

{"the sight is a more important thing than the drawing"}

[. . .] I am nearly convinced, that when once we see keenly enough, there is very little difficulty in drawing what we see; but, even supposing that this difficulty be still great, I believe that the sight is a more important thing than the drawing; and I would rather teach drawing that my pupils may learn to love Nature, than teach the looking at Nature that they may learn to draw. It is surely also a more important thing, for young people and unprofessional students, to know how to appreciate the art of others, than to gain much power in art themselves. Now the modes of sketching ordinarily taught are inconsistent with this power of judgment. No person trained to the superficial execution of modern water-colour painting, can understand the work of Titian or Leonardo; they must forever remain blind to the refinement of such men's penciling, and the precision of their thinking. But, however slight a degree of manipulative power the student may reach by pursuing the mode recommended to him in these letters, I will answer for it that he cannot go once through the advised exercises without beginning to understand what masterly work means; and, by the time he has gained some proficiency in them, he will have a pleasure in looking at the painting of the great schools, and a new perception of the exquisiteness of natural scenery, such as would repay him for much more labor than I have asked him to undergo.

—*The Elements of Drawing*, Preface (1857)

★

{"No great painters ever trouble themselves about perspective"}

No great painters ever trouble themselves about perspective, and very few of them know its laws; they draw everything by the eye, and, naturally enough, disdain in the easy parts of their work rules which cannot help them in difficult ones. It would take about a month's labor to draw imperfectly, by laws of perspective, what any great Venetian will draw perfectly in five minutes, when he is throwing a wreath of leaves round a head, or bending the curves of a pattern in and out among the folds of drapery. It is true that when perspective was first discovered, everybody amused themselves with it; and all the great painters put fine saloons and arcades behind their Madonnas, merely to show that they could draw in perspective: but even this was generally done by them only to catch the public eye, and they disdained the perspective so much, that though they took the greatest pains with the circlet of a crown, or the rim of a crystal cup, in the heart of their picture, they would twist their capitals of columns and towers of churches about in the background in the most wanton way, wherever they liked the lines to go, provided only they left just perspective enough to please the public.

In modern days, I doubt if any artist among us, except David Roberts, knows so much perspective as would enable him to draw a Gothic arch to scale at a given angle and distance. Turner, though he was professor of perspective to the Royal Academy, did not know what he professed, and never, as far as I remember, drew a single building in true perspective in his life; he drew them only with as much perspective as suited him. Prout also knew nothing of perspective, and twisted his buildings, as Turner did, into whatever shapes he liked. I do not justify this; and would recommend the student at least to treat perspective with common civility, but to pay no court to it.

—*The Elements of Drawing*, Preface (1857)

★

{"Nothing is of the least use to young people [. . .] but what interests them"}

[. . .] the works of the great masters can only be serviceable to the student after he has made considerable progress himself. It only wastes the time and dulls the feelings of young persons, to drag them through picture galleries; at least, unless they themselves wish to look at particular pictures. Generally, young people only care to enter a picture gallery when there is a chance of getting leave to run a race to the other end of it; and they had better do that in the garden below. If, however, they have any real enjoyment of pictures, and want to look at this one or that, the principal point is never to disturb them in looking at what interests them, and never to make them look at what does not. Nothing is of the least use to young people (nor, by the way, of much use to old ones), but what interests them; and therefore, though it is of great importance to put nothing but good art into their possession, yet, when they are passing through great houses or galleries, they should be allowed to look precisely at what pleases them: if it is not useful to them as art, it will be in some other way; and the healthiest way in which art can interest them is when they look at it, not as art, but because it represents something they like in Nature. If a boy has had his heart filled by the life of some great man, and goes up thirstily to a Van Dyck portrait of him, to see what he was like, that is the wholesomest way in which he can begin the study of portraiture; if he loves mountains, and dwells on a Turner drawing because he sees in it a likeness to a Yorkshire scar or an Alpine pass, that is the wholesomest way in which he can begin the study of landscape; and if a girl's mind is filled with dreams of angels and saints, and she pauses before an Angelico because she thinks it must surely be like heaven, that is the right way for her to begin the study of religious art.

—*The Elements of Drawing*, Appendix, "Things to Be Studied" (1857)

★

{"knowing the way things are going"}

Now remember, nothing distinguishes great men from inferior men more than their always, whether in life or in art, *knowing the way things are going*. Your dunce thinks they are standing still, and draws them all fixed; your wise man sees the change or changing in them, and draws them so,—the animal in its motion, the tree in its growth, the cloud in its course, the mountain in its wearing away. Try always, whenever you look at a form, to see the lines in it which have had power over its past fate and will have power over its futurity. Those are its *awful* lines; see that you seize on those, whatever else you miss.

—*The Elements of Drawing*, "Sketching from Nature" (1857)

★

{"That leaf is of such and such a character"}

The noble draughtsman draws a leaf, and stops, and says calmly,—That leaf is of such and such a character; I will give him a friend who will entirely suit him: then he considers what his friend ought to be, and having determined, he draws his friend. This process may be as quick as lightning when the master is great—one of the sons of the giants; or it may be slow and timid: but the process is always gone through; no touch or form is ever added to another by a good painter without a mental determination and affirmation. But when the hand has got into a habit, leaf No. 1 necessitates leaf No. 2; you cannot stop, your hand is as a horse with the bit in its teeth; or rather is, for the time, a machine, throwing out leaves to order and pattern, all alike. You must stop that hand of yours, however painfully; make it understand that it is not to have its own way any more, that it shall never more slip from one touch to another without orders; otherwise it is not you who are the master, but your fingers. You may therefore study Harding's drawing, and take pleasure in it; and you may properly admire the dexterity which applies the habit of the hand so well, and produces results on the whole so satisfactory: but you must never copy it; otherwise your progress will be at once arrested. The utmost you can ever hope to do would be a sketch in Harding's manner, but of far inferior dexterity; for he has given his life's toil to gain his dexterity, and you, I suppose, have other things to work at besides drawing. You would also incapacitate yourself from ever understanding what truly great work was, or what Nature was; but, by the earnest and complete study of facts, you will gradually come to understand the one and love the other more and more, whether you can draw well yourself or not.

I have yet to say a few words respecting the third law above stated, that of mystery; the law, namely, that nothing is ever seen perfectly, but only by fragments, and under various conditions of obscurity. This last fact renders the visible objects of Nature complete as a type of the human nature. We have, observe, first, Subordination; secondly, Individuality; lastly, and this not the least essential character, Incomprehensibility; a perpetual lesson, in every serrated point and shining vein which escapes or deceives our sight among the forest leaves, how little we may hope to discern clearly, or judge justly, the rents and veins of the human heart; how much of all that is round us, in men's actions or spirits, which we at first think we understand, a closer and more loving watchfulness would show to be full of mystery, never to be either fathomed or withdrawn.

—*The Elements of Drawing*, "Sketching from Nature" (1857)

★

{"when you are fairly *at* the work, what is the motive then which tells upon every touch of it?"}

All of you have the trial of yourselves in your own power; each may undergo at this instant, before his own judgment seat, the ordeal by fire. Ask yourselves what is the leading motive which actuates you while you are at work. I do not ask you what your leading motive is for working—that is a different thing; you may have families to support—parents to help—brides to win; you may have all these, or other such sacred and pre-eminent motives, to press the morning's labour and prompt the twilight thought. But when you are fairly *at* the work, what is the motive then which tells upon every touch of it? If it is the love of that which your work represents—if, being a landscape painter, it is love of hills and trees that moves you—if, being a figure painter, it is love of human beauty and human soul that moves you—if, being a flower or animal painter, it is love, and wonder, and delight in petal and in limb that move you, then the Spirit is upon you, and the earth is yours, and the fulness thereof. But if, on the other hand, it is petty self-complacency in your own skill, trust in precepts and laws, hope for academical or popular approbation, or avarice of wealth,—it is quite possible that by steady industry, or even by fortunate chance, you may win the applause, the position, the fortune, that you desire;—but one touch of true art you will never lay on canvas or on stone as long as you live. Make, then, your choice, boldly and consciously, for one way or other it *must* be made. On the dark and dangerous side are set, the pride which delights in self-contemplation—the indolence which rests in unquestioned forms—the ignorance that despises what is fairest among God's creatures, and the dulness that denies what is marvellous in His working: there is a life of monotony for your own souls, and of misguiding for those of others. And, on the other side, is open to your choice the life of the crowned spirit, moving as a light in creation—discovering always—illuminating always, gaining every hour in strength, yet bowed down every hour into deeper humility; sure of being right in its aim, sure of being irresistible in its progress; happy in what it has securely done—happier in what, day by day, it may as securely hope; happiest at the close of life, when the right hand begins to forget its cunning, to remember, that there never was a touch of the chisel or the pencil it wielded, but has added to the knowledge and quickened the happiness of mankind.[26]

—*The Two Paths*, "The Deteriorative Power of Conventional Art Over Nations" (1858)

★

{"If you paint as you ought, and study as you ought, depend upon it the public will take no notice of you for a long while"}

[. . .] it follows that since Manufacture is simply the operation of the hand of man in producing that which is useful to him, it essentially separates itself from the emotions; when emotions interfere with machinery they spoil it: machinery must go evenly, without emotion. But the Fine Arts cannot go evenly; they always must have emotion ruling their mechanism, and until the pupil begins to feel, and until all he does associates itself with the current of his feeling, he is not an artist. But pupils in all the schools in this country are now exposed to all kinds of temptations which blunt their feelings. I constantly feel discouraged in addressing them because I know not how to tell

[26] John Ruskin, *Arch from the Façade of the Church of San Michele*, 1849, sketch.

them boldly what they ought to do, when I feel how practically difficult it is for them to do it. There are all sorts of demands made upon them in every direction, and money is to be made in every conceivable way but the right way. If you paint as you ought, and study as you ought, depend upon it the public will take no notice of you for a long while. If you study wrongly, and try to draw the attention of the public upon you,—supposing you to be clever students—you will get swift reward; but the reward does not come fast when it is sought wisely; it is always held aloof for a little while; the right roads of early life are very quiet ones, hedged in from nearly all help or praise. But the wrong roads are noisy,—vociferous everywhere with all kinds of demands upon you for art which is not properly art at all; and in the various meetings of modern interests, money is to be made in every way; but art is to be followed only in *one* way.

—*The Two Paths*, "The Unity of Art" (1858)

★

{"if we have the power of showing them the best thing, we should show them the best thing"}

Now the question is, whether, as students, we are to study only these mightiest men, who unite all greatness, or whether we are to study the works of inferior men, who present us with the greatness which we particularly like? That question often comes before me when I see a strong idiosyncrasy in a student, and he asks me what he should study. Shall I send him to a true master, who does not present the quality in a prominent way in which that student delights, or send him to a man with whom he has direct sympathy? It is a hard question. For very curious results have sometimes been brought out, especially in late years, not only by students following their own bent, but by their being withdrawn from teaching altogether. I have just named a very great man in his own field—Prout. We all know his drawings, and love them: they have a peculiar character which no other architectural drawings ever possessed, and which no others can possess, because all Prout's subjects are being knocked down or restored. (Prout did not like restored buildings any more than I do.) There will never be any more Prout drawings. Nor could he have been what he was, or expressed with that mysteriously effective touch that peculiar delight in broken and old buildings, unless he had been withdrawn from all high art influence. You know that Prout was born of poor parents—that he was educated down in Cornwall;—and that, for many years, all the art-teaching he had was his own, or the fishermen's. Under the keels of the fishing-boats, on the sands of our southern coasts, Prout learned all that he needed to learn about art. Entirely by himself, he felt his way to this particular style, and became the painter of pictures which I think we should all regret to lose. It becomes a very difficult question what that man would have been, had he been brought under some entirely wholesome artistic influence. He had immense gifts of composition. I do not know any man who had more power of invention than Prout, or who had a sublimer instinct in his treatment of things; but being entirely withdrawn from all artistical help, he blunders his way to that short-coming representation, which, by the very reason of its short-coming, has a certain charm we should all be sorry to lose.[27] And therefore I feel embarrassed when a student comes to me, in whom I see a strong instinct of that kind: and cannot tell whether I ought to say to him, "Give up all your studies of old boats, and keep away from the sea-shore, and come up to the Royal Academy in London, and look at nothing but Titian." It is a difficult thing to make up one's mind to say that. However, I believe, on the whole, we may wisely leave such matters in the hands of Providence; that if we have the power of teaching the right to anybody, we should teach them the right; if we have the power of showing them the best thing, we should show them the best thing; there will always, I fear, be enough want of teaching, and enough bad teaching, to bring out very curious erratical results if we want them. So, if we are to teach at all, let us teach the right thing, and ever the right thing.

—*The Two Paths*, "The Unity of Art" (1858)

★

{"There's no way of getting good Art, I repeat, but one"}

If you want really good work, such as will be acknowledged by all the world, there is but one way of getting it, and that is a difficult one. You may offer any premium you choose for it—but you will find it can't be done for premiums. You may send for patterns to the

[27] Samuel Prout, *Coastal Scene with Beached Boats in Foreground*, early-mid nineteenth century, painting.

antipodes—but you will find it can't be done upon patterns. You may lecture on the principles of Art to every school in the kingdom—and you will find it can't be done upon principles. You may wait patiently for the progress of the age—and you will find your Art is unprogressive. Or you may set yourselves impatiently to urge it by the inventions of the age—and you will find your chariot of Art entirely immovable either by screw or paddle. There's no way of getting good Art, I repeat, but one—at once the simplest and the most difficult—namely, to enjoy it. Examine the history of nations, and you will find this great fact clear and unmistakable on the front of it—that good Art has only been produced by nations who rejoiced in it; fed themselves with it, as if it were bread; basked in it, as if it were sunshine; shouted at the sight of it; danced with the delight of it; quarreled for it; fought for it; starved for it; did, in fact, precisely the opposite with it of what we want to do with it—they made it to keep and we to sell.

—"Inaugural Address Delivered at the Cambridge School of Art" (1858)

★

{"The object of the great Resemblant Arts is, and always has been, to resemble"}

All second-rate artists—(and remember, the second-rate ones are a loquacious multitude, while the great come only one or two in a century; and then, silently)—all second-rate artists will tell you that the object of fine art is not resemblance, but some kind of abstraction more refined than reality. Put that out of your heads at once. The object of the great Resemblant Arts is, and always has been, to resemble; and to resemble as closely as possible. It is the function of a good portrait to set the man before you in habit as he lived, and I would we had a few more that did so. It is the function of a good landscape to set the scene before you in its reality; to make you, if it may be, think the clouds are flying, and the streams foaming. It is the function of the best sculptor—the true Dædalus—to make stillness look like breathing, and marble look like flesh.

And in all great times of art, this purpose is as naïvely expressed as it is steadily held. All the talk about abstraction belongs to periods of decadence. In living times, people see something living that pleases them; and they try to make it live forever, or to make something as like it as possible, that will last forever. They paint their statues, and inlay the eyes with jewels, and set real crowns on the heads; they finish, in their pictures, every thread of embroidery, and would fain, if they could, draw every leaf upon the trees. And their only verbal expression of conscious success is that they have made their work "look real."

You think all that very wrong. So did I, once; but it was I that was wrong. A long time ago, before ever I had seen Oxford, I painted a picture of the Lake of Como, for my father. It was not at all like the Lake of Como; but I thought it rather the better for that. My father differed with me; and objected particularly to a boat with a red and yellow awning, which I had put into the most conspicuous corner of my drawing. I declared this boat to be "necessary to the composition." My father not the less objected, that he had never seen such a boat, either at Como or elsewhere; and suggested that if I would make the lake look a little more like water, I should be under no necessity of explaining its nature by the presence of floating objects. I thought him at the time a very simple person for his pains; but have since learned, and it is the very gist of all practical matters, which, as Professor of Fine Art, I have now to tell you, that the great point in painting a lake is—to get it to look like water.

So far, so good. We lay it down for a first principle that our graphic art, whether painting or sculpture, is to produce something which shall look as like Nature as possible. But now we must go one step farther, and say that it is to produce what shall look like Nature to people who know what Nature is like! You see this is at once a great restriction, as well as a great exaltation of our aim. Our business is not to deceive the simple; but to deceive the wise!

—*Arata Pentelici*, "Likeness" (1870)

★

{"you never will love art well, till you love what she mirrors better"}

There is nothing that I tell you with more eager desire that you should believe—nothing with wider ground in my experience for requiring you to believe, than this, that you never will love art well, till you love what she mirrors better.

It is the widest, as the clearest experience I have to give you; for the beginning of all my own right art work in life, (and it may not be unprofitable that I should tell you this,) depended not on my love of art, but of mountains and sea. All boys with any good in them are fond of boats, and of course I liked the mountains best when they had lakes at the bottom; and I used to walk always in the middle of the loosest gravel I could find in the roads of the midland counties, that I might hear, as I trod on it, something like the sound of the pebbles on sea-beach. No chance occurred for some time to develop what gift of drawing I had; but I would pass entire days in rambling on the Cumberland hillsides, or staring at the lines of surf on a low sand; and when I was taken annually to the Water-colour Exhibition, I used to get hold of a catalogue before-hand, mark all the Robsons, which I knew would be of purple mountains, and all the Copley Fieldings, which I knew would be of lakes or sea; and then go deliberately round the room to these, for the sake, observe, not of the pictures, in any wise, but only of the things painted.

And through the whole of following life, whatever power of judgment I have obtained, in art, which I am now confident and happy in using, or communicating, has depended on my steady habit of always looking for the subject principally, and for the art, only as the means of expressing it.

—*The Eagle's Nest*, "The Relation of Wise Art to Wise Science" (1872)

★

{". . . in art, as in life, it depends mainly on simplicity of purpose"}

An artist's nerve and power of mind are lost chiefly in deciding what to do, and in effacing what he has done: it is anxiety, not labor, that fatigues him; and vacillation, not difficulty that hinders him. And if the student feels doubt respecting his own decision of mind, and questions the possibility of gaining the habit of it, let him be assured that in art, as in life, it depends mainly on simplicity of purpose. Turner's decision came chiefly of his truthfulness; it was because he meant always to be true, that he was able always to be bold. And you will find that you may gain his courage, if you will maintain his fidelity. If you want only to make your drawing fine, or attractive, you may hesitate indeed, long and often, to consider whether your faults will be forgiven, or your fineries perceived. But if you want to put fair fact into it, you will find the fact shape it fairly for you; and that in pictures, no less in human life, they who have once made up their minds to do right, will have little place for hesitation, and little cause for repentance.

—*The Laws of Fesole*, "Of the Relation of Colour to Outline" (1877)

★

{"all true art is praise"}

The art of man is the expression of his rational and disciplined delight in the forms and laws of the creation of which he forms a part. [. . .]

[. . .] all true art is praise.

There is no exception to this great law [. . .]

Fix, then, this in your mind as the guiding principle of all right practical labor, and source of all healthful life energy, that your art is to be the praise of something that you love. It may be only the praise of a shell or a stone; it may be the praise of a hero; it may be the praise of God: your rank as a living creature is determined by the height and breadth of your love; but, be you small or great, what healthy art is possible to you must be the expression of your true delight in a real thing, better than the art. [. . .]

This is the main lesson I have been teaching, so far as I have been able, through my whole life: Only that picture is noble, which is painted in love of the reality. It is a law which embraces the highest scope of Art; it is one also which guides in security the first steps of it. If you desire to draw, that you may represent something that you care for, you will advance swiftly and safely. If you desire to draw, that you may make a beautiful drawing, you will never make one.

—*The Laws of Fesole*, "All Great Art Is Praise" (1877)

Sculpture and Architecture

{"The sculptor must paint with his chisel"}

I AM NOT sure whether it is frequently enough observed that sculpture is not the mere cutting of the *form* of anything in stone; it is the cutting of the *effect* of it. Very often the true form, in the marble, would not be in the least like itself. The sculptor must paint with his chisel: half his touches are not to realize, but to put power into the form: they are touches of light and shadow; and raise a ridge, or sink a hollow, not to represent an actual ridge or hollow, but to get a line of light, or a spot of darkness. In a coarse way, this kind of execution is very marked in old French woodwork; the irises of the eyes of its chimeric monsters being cut boldly into holes, which, variously placed, and always dark, give all kinds of strange and startling expressions, averted and askance, to the fantastic countenances. Perhaps the highest examples of this kind of sculpture-painting are the works of Mino da Fiesole; their best effects being reached by strange angular, and seemingly rude, touches of the chisel. The lips of one of the children on the tombs in the church of the Badia, appear only half finished when they are seen close; yet the expression is farther carried and more ineffable, than in any piece of marble I have ever seen, especially considering its delicacy, and the softness of the child-features.

—*The Seven Lamps of Architecture*, "The Lamp of Life" (1849)

★

{"The man who has eye and intellect will invent beautiful proportions"}

Proportions are as infinite (and that in all kinds of things, as severally in colours, lines, shades, lights, and forms) as possible airs in music:

and it is just as rational an attempt to teach a young architect how to proportion truly and well by calculating for him the proportions of fine works, as it would be to teach him to compose melodies by calculating the mathematical relations of the notes in Beethoven's *Adelaide* or Mozart's *Requiem.* The man who has eye and intellect will invent beautiful proportions, and cannot help it; but he can no more tell *us* how to do it than Wordsworth could tell us how to write a sonnet, or than Scott could have told us how to plan a romance.

—*The Seven Lamps of Architecture*,
"The Lamp of Beauty" (1849)

★

{"however long you gaze at this simple ornament [. . .] you are never weary of it"}

[. . .] he was no common man who designed that cathedral of Dunblane. I know not anything so perfect in its simplicity, and so beautiful, as far as it reaches, in all the Gothic with which I am acquainted. And just in proportion to his power of mind, that man was content to work under Nature's teaching; and instead of putting a merely formal dogtooth, as everybody else did at the time, he went down to the woody bank of the sweet river beneath the rocks on which he was building, and he took up a few of the fallen leaves that lay by it, and he set them in his arch, side by side, forever. And, look—that he might show you he had done this,—he has made them all of different sizes, just as they lay; and that you might not by any chance miss noticing the variety, he has put a great broad one at the top, and then a little one turned the wrong way, next to it, so that you must be blind indeed if you do not understand his meaning. And the healthy change and playfulness of this just does in the stone-work what it does on the tree boughs, and is a perpetual refreshment and invigoration; so that, however long you gaze at this simple ornament—and none can be simpler, a village mason could carve it all round the window in a few hours—you are never weary of it, it seems always new.

—*Lectures on Architecture and Painting*, "Architecture" (1853)

★

{"*the demand for perfection is always a sign of a misunderstanding of the ends of art*"}

It seems a fantastic paradox, but it is nevertheless a most important truth, that no architecture can be truly noble which is *not* imperfect. And this is easily demonstrable. For since the architect, whom we will suppose capable of doing all in perfection, cannot execute the whole with his own hands, he must either make slaves of his workmen in the old Greek, and present English fashion, and level his work to a slave's capacities, which is to degrade it; or else he must take his workmen as he finds them, and let them show their weaknesses together with their strength, which will involve the Gothic imperfection, but render the whole work as noble as the intellect of the age can make it.

But the principle may be stated more broadly still. I have confined the illustration of it to architecture, but I must not leave it as if true of architecture only. Hitherto I have used the words imperfect and perfect merely to distinguish between work grossly unskillful, and work executed with average precision and science; and I have been pleading that any degree of unskillfulness should be admitted, so only that the laborer's mind had room for expression. But, accurately speaking, no good work whatever can be perfect, and *the demand for perfection is always a sign of a misunderstanding of the ends of art.*

This for two reasons, both based on everlasting laws. The first, that no great man ever stops working till he has reached his point of failure; that is to say, his mind is always far in advance of his powers of execution, and the latter will now and then give way in trying to follow it; besides that he will always give to the inferior portions of his work only such inferior attention as they require; and according to his greatness he becomes accustomed to the feeling of dissatisfaction with the best he can do, that in moments of lassitude or anger with himself he will not care though the beholder be dissatisfied also. I believe there has only been one man who would not acknowledge this necessity, and strove always to reach perfection, Leonardo; the end of his vain effort being merely that he would take ten years to a picture, and leave it unfinished. And therefore, if we are to have great men working at all, or less men doing their best, the work will be imperfect, however beautiful. Of human work none but what is bad can be perfect, in its own bad way.

—*The Stones of Venice*, Vol. II, "The Nature of Gothic" (1853)

★

{"see that your work is easily and happily done, else it will never make anybody else happy"}

[. . .] what a peculiar importance, and responsibility, are attached to your work, when you consider its permanence, and the multitudes to whom it is addressed. We frequently are led, by wise people, to consider what responsibility may sometimes attach to words, which yet, the chance is, will be heard by few, and forgotten as soon as heard. But none of *your w*ords will be heard by few, and none will be forgotten, for five or six hundred years, if you build well. You will talk to all who pass by; and all those little sympathies, those freaks of fancy, those jests in stone, those workings-out of problems in caprice, will occupy mind after mind of utterly countless multitudes, long after you are gone. You have not, like authors, to plead for a hearing, or to fear oblivion. Do but build large enough, and carve boldly enough, and all the world will hear you; they cannot choose but look.

I do not mean to awe you by this thought; I do not mean that because you will have so many witnesses and watchers, you are never to jest, or do anything gaily or lightly; on the contrary, I have pleaded, from the beginning, for this art of yours, especially because it has room for the whole of your character—if jest is in you, let the jest be jested; if mathematical ingenuity is yours, let your problem be put, and your solution worked out, as quaintly as you choose; above all, see that your work is easily and happily done, else it will never make anybody else happy; but while you thus give the rein to all your impulses, see that those impulses be headed and centred by one noble impulse; and let that be Love—triple love—for the art which you practise, the creation in which you move, and the creatures to whom you minister.

—*The Two Paths*, "Influence of Imagination in Architecture" (1858)

★

{"sculpture [. . .] is an irresistible human instinct for the making of cats and mice"}

Some years ago, having been always desirous that the education of women should begin in learning how to cook, I got leave, one day, for a little girl of eleven years old to exchange, much to her satisfaction, her schoolroom for the kitchen. But as ill-fortune would have it, there was some pastry toward, and she was left unadvisedly in command of some delicately rolled paste; whereof she made no pies, but an unlimited quantity of cats and mice.

Now you may read the works of the gravest critics of art from end to end; but you will find, at last, they can give you no other true account of the spirit of sculpture than that it is an irresistible human instinct for the making of cats and mice, and other imitable living creatures, in such permanent form that one may play with the images at leisure. Play with them, or love them, or fear them, or worship them. The cat may become the goddess Pasht, and the mouse, in the hand of a sculptured king, enforce his enduring words "ἐς ἐμέ τις ὁρέων εὐσεβὴς ἔστω"[28]; but the great mimetic instinct underlies all such purpose; and is zooplastic,—life-shaping,—alike in the reverent and the impious. [. . .]

If my little lady in the kitchen had been put in command of colours, as well as of dough, and if the paste would have taken the colours, we may be sure her mice would have been painted brown, and her cats tortoiseshell; and this, partly indeed for the added delight and prettiness of colour itself, but more for the sake of absolute realization to her eyes and mind. Now all the early sculpture of the most accomplished nations has been thus coloured, rudely or finely; and therefore you see at once how necessary it is that we should keep the term "graphic" for imitative art generally; since no separation can at first be made between carving and painting, with reference to the mental powers exerted in, or addressed by, them. In the earliest known art of the world, a reindeer hunt may be scratched in outline on the flat side of a clean-picked bone, and a reindeer's head carved out of the end of it; both these are flint-knife work, and, strictly speaking, sculpture: but the scratched outline is the beginning of drawing, and the carved head of sculpture proper. When the spaces

[28] Greek: *es eme tis horeôn eusebês estô*: "Let the one looking at me be reverent." A thank-you to Michael Gilleland for that translation; he notes that Ruskin is quoting the historian Herodotus. See Gilleland's blog, "Laudatator Temporis Acti."

inclosed by the scratched outline are filled with colour, the colouring soon becomes a principal means of effect [. . .].

And now observe that, while the graphic arts begin in the mere mimetic effort, they proceed, as they obtain more perfect realization, to act under the influence of a stronger and higher instinct. They begin by scratching the reindeer, the most interesting object of sight. But presently, as the human creature rises in scale of intellect, it proceeds to scratch, not the most interesting object of sight only, but the most interesting object of imagination; not the reindeer, but the Maker and Giver of the reindeer. And the second great condition for the advance of the art of sculpture is that the race should possess, in addition to the mimetic instinct, the realistic or idolizing instinct; the desire to see as substantial the powers that are unseen, and bring near those that are far off, and to possess and cherish those that are strange. To make in some way tangible and visible the nature of the gods—to illustrate and explain it by symbols; to bring the immortals out of the recesses of the clouds, and make them Penates; to bring back the dead from darkness, and make them Lares.[29]

Our conception of this tremendous and universal human passion has been altogether narrowed by the current idea that Pagan religious art consisted only, or chiefly, in giving personality to the gods. The personality was never doubted; it was visibility, interpretation, and possession that the hearts of men sought.

—*Arata Pentelici*, "Idolatry" (1870)

★

{"our requirement of the finest art [. . .] that it shall be so like the thing it represents as to please those who best know or can conceive the original"}

[. . .] you will feel that, lovely as the drawing is, you would like far better to see the real place, and the goats skipping among the rocks, and the spray floating above the fall. And this is the true sign of the greatest art—to part voluntarily with its greatness;—to make *itself* poor and unnoticed; but so to exalt and set forth its theme, that you may be fain to see the theme instead of it. So that you have never enough admired a great workman's doing, till you have begun to despise it. The best homage that could be paid to the *Athena* of Phidias

[29] Penates and Lares are household gods.

would be to desire rather to see the living goddess; and the loveliest Madonnas of Christian art fall short of their due power, if they do not make their beholders sick at heart to see the living Virgin.

We have then, for our requirement of the finest art, (sculpture, or anything else,) that it shall be so like the thing it represents as to please those who best know or can conceive the original; and, if possible, please them deceptively—its final triumph being to deceive even the wise; and (the Greeks thought) to please even the Immortals, who were so wise as to be undeceivable. So that you get the Greek, thus far entirely true, idea of perfectness in sculpture, expressed to you by what Phalaris says, at first sight of the bull of Perilaus, "It only wanted motion and bellowing to seem alive; and as soon as I saw it, I cried out, it ought to be sent to the god,"—to Apollo, for only he, the undeceivable, could thoroughly understand such sculpture, and perfectly delight in it.

—*Arata Pentelici*, "Likeness" (1870)

J. M. W. Turner

{"He had, of course, the usual difficulties of young artists to encounter"}

[. . .] TURNER DIFFERED FROM most men in this,—that he was always willing to take anything to do that came in his way. He did not shut himself up in a garret to produce unsaleable works of "high art," and starve, or lose his senses. He hired himself out every evening to wash in skies in Indian ink, on other people's drawings, as many as he could, at half-a-crown a-night, getting his supper into the bargain. "What could I have done better?" he said afterwards: "it was first-rate practice." Then he took to illustrating guide-books and almanacks, and anything that wanted cheap frontispieces. [. . .]

There was another great difference between Turner and other men. In doing these drawings for the commonest publications of the day, and for a remuneration, altogether contemptible, he never did his work badly because he thought it beneath him, or because he was ill-paid. There does not exist such a thing as a slovenly drawing by Turner. With what people were willing to give him for his work he was content; but he considered that work in its relation to himself, not in its relation to the purchaser. He took a poor price, that he might *live*; but he made noble drawings, that he might *learn*. Of course some are slighter than others, and they vary in their materials; those executed with pencil and Indian ink being never finished to the degree of those which are executed in colour. But he is *never* careless. According to the time and means at his disposal, he always did his best. He never let a drawing leave his hands without having made a step in advance, and having done better in it than he had ever done before; and there is no important drawing of the period which is not executed with a *total* disregard of time and price, and which was not, even then, worth four or five times what Turner received for it.

—*Lectures on Architecture and Painting*, "Turner and His Works" (1853)

★

{"the only painter [. . .] who has ever drawn the sky"}

[. . .] it may be generally stated that Turner is the only painter, so far as I know, who has ever drawn the sky, (not the clear sky, which we before saw belonged exclusively to the religious schools, but the various forms and phenomena of the cloudy heavens,) all previous artists having only represented it typically or partially; but he absolutely and universally: he is the only painter who has ever drawn a mountain, or a stone; no other man ever having learned their organization, or possessed himself of their spirit, except in part and obscurely (the one or two stones noted of Tintoret's [*Modern Painters* Vol. II., Part III., Ch. 3] are perhaps hardly enough on which to found an exception in his favor.) He is the only painter who ever drew the stem of a tree, Titian having come the nearest before him, and excelling him in the muscular development of the larger trunks, (though sometimes losing the woody strength in a serpent-like flaccidity,) but missing the grace and character of the ramifications. He is the only painter who has ever represented the surface of calm, or the force of agitated water; who has represented the effects of space on distant objects, or who has rendered the abstract beauty of natural colour. These assertions I make deliberately, after careful weighing and consideration, in no spirit of dispute, or momentary zeal; but from strong and convinced feeling, and with the consciousness of being able to prove them.

—*Modern Painters*, Vol. I, "Recapitulation" (1843)

★

{"why [. . .] do you blame Turner because he dazzles you?"}

[. . .] it is singular enough that the chief attacks on Turner for overcharged brilliancy, are made, not when there could by any possibility be any chance of his outstepping nature, but when he has taken subjects which no colours of earth could ever vie with or reach, such, for instance, as his sunsets among the high clouds. When I come to speak of skies, I shall point out what divisions, proportioned to their elevation, exist in the character of clouds. It is the highest region,—that exclusively characterized by white, filmy, multitudinous, and quiet clouds, arranged in bars, or streaks, or flakes, of which I speak at present, a region which no landscape painters have ever made one effort to represent, except Rubens and Turner—the latter taking it for his most favorite and frequent study. Now we have been speaking hitherto of what is constant and necessary in nature, of the ordinary effects of daylight on ordinary colours, and we repeat again, that no gorgeousness of the pallet can reach even these. But it is a widely different thing when nature herself takes a colouring fit, and does something extraordinary, something really to exhibit her power. She has a thousand ways and means of rising above herself, but incomparably the noblest manifestations of her capability of colour are in these sunsets among the high clouds. I speak especially of the moment before the sun sinks, when his light turns pure rose-colour, and when this light falls upon a zenith covered with countless cloud-forms of inconceivable delicacy, threads and flakes of vapor, which would in common daylight be pure snow white, and which give therefore fair field to the tone of light. There is then no limit to the multitude, and no check to the intensity of the hues assumed. The whole sky from the zenith to the horizon becomes one molten, mantling sea of colour and fire; every black bar turns into massy gold, every ripple and wave into unsullied, shadowless, crimson, and purple, and scarlet, and colours for which there are no words in language, and no ideas in the mind,—things which can only be conceived while they are visible,—the intense hollow blue of the upper sky melting through it all,—showing here deep, and pure, and lightless, there, modulated by the filmy, formless body of the transparent vapor, till it is lost imperceptibly in its crimson and gold. Now there is no connection, no one link of association or resemblance, between those skies and the work of any mortal hand but Turner's. He alone has followed nature in these her highest efforts; he follows her faithfully, but far behind; follows at such a distance below her intensity that the *Napoleon* of last year's exhibition, and the Temeraire of the year before, would look colourless and cold if the eye came upon them after one of nature's sunsets among the high clouds. [. . .]

Even granting the constant vigor of observation, and supposing the possession of such impossible knowledge, it needs but a moment's reflection to prove how incapable the memory is of retaining for any time the distinct image of the sources even of its most vivid impressions. What recollection have we of the sunsets which delighted us last year? We may know that they were magnificent, or glowing, but no distinct image of colour or form is retained—nothing of whose *degree* (for the great difficulty with the memory is to retain, not facts, but *degrees* of fact) we could be so certain as to say of anything now presented to us, that it is like it. If we did say so, we should be wrong; for we may be quite certain that the energy of an impression fades from the memory, and becomes more and more indistinct every day; and thus we compare a faded and indistinct image with the decision and certainty of one present to the senses. How constantly do we affirm that the thunder-storm of last week was the most terrible one we ever saw in our lives, because we compare it, not with the thunder-storm of last year, but with the faded and feeble recollection of it. And so, when we enter an exhibition, as we have no definite standard of truth before us, our feelings are toned down and subdued to the quietness of colour which is all that human power can ordinarily attain to; and when we turn to a piece of higher and closer truth, approaching the pitch of the colour of nature, but to which we are not guided, as we should be in nature, by corresponding gradations of light everywhere around us, but which is isolated and cut off suddenly by a frame and a wall, and surrounded by darkness and coldness, what can we expect but that it should surprise and shock the feelings? Suppose, where the Napoleon hung in the Academy last year, there could have been left, instead, an opening in the wall, and through that opening, in the midst of the obscurity of the dim room and the smoke-laden atmosphere, there could suddenly have been poured the full glory of a tropical sunset, reverberated from the sea: How would you have shrunk, blinded, from its scarlet and intolerable lightnings! What picture in the room would not have been blackness after it? And why then do you blame Turner because he dazzles you? Does not the falsehood rest with those who do *not*? There was not one hue in this whole picture which was not far below what nature would have used in the same circumstances, nor was there one inharmonious or at variance with the rest;—the stormy blood-red of the horizon, the scarlet of the breaking sunlight, the rich crimson browns of the wet and illumined sea-weed; the pure gold and purple of the upper sky, and, shed through it all, the deep passage of solemn blue, where the cold moonlight fell on one pensive spot of the limitless shore—all were given with harmony as perfect as their colour was intense; and if, instead of passing, as I doubt not you did, in the hurry of your unreflecting prejudice, you had paused but so much as one quarter of an hour before the picture, you would have found the sense of air and space blended with every line, and breathing in every cloud, and every colour instinct and radiant with visible, glowing, absorbing light.

—*Modern Painters*, Vol. I, "Of Truth of Colour" (1843)

★

{"He obtains this expression of force in falling or running water by fearless and full rendering of its forms"}

It will be remembered that it was said above, that Turner was the only painter who had ever represented the surface of calm or the *force* of agitated water. He obtains this expression of force in falling or running water by fearless and full rendering of its forms. He never loses himself and his subject in the splash of the fall—his presence of mind never fails as he goes down; he does not blind us with the spray, or veil the countenance of his fall with its own drapery. A little crumbling white, or lightly rubbed paper, will soon give the effect of indiscriminate foam; but nature gives more than foam—she shows beneath it, and through it, a peculiar character of exquisitely studied form bestowed on every wave and line of fall; and it is this variety of definite character which Turner always aims at, rejecting, as much as possible, everything that conceals or overwhelms it. Thus, in the *Upper Fall of the Tees*, though the whole basin of the fall is blue and dim with the rising vapor, yet the whole attention of the spectator is directed to that which it was peculiarly difficult to render, the concentric zones and delicate curves of the falling water itself; and it is impossible to express with what exquisite accuracy these are given. They are the characteristic of a powerful stream descending without impediment or break, but from a narrow channel, so as to expand as it falls. They are the constant form which such a stream assumes as it descends; and yet I think it would be difficult to point to another instance of their being rendered in art. You will find nothing in the waterfalls even of our best painters, but springing lines of parabolic descent, and splashing, shapeless foam; and, in consequence, though they may make you understand the swiftness of the water, they never let you feel the weight of it; the stream in their hands looks *active*, not *supine*, as if it leaped, not as if it fell. Now water will leap a little way, it will leap down a weir or over a stone, but it *tumbles* over a high fall like this; and it is when we have lost the parabolic line, and arrived at the catenary,—when we have lost the *spring* of the fall, and arrived at the *plunge* of it, that we begin really to feel its weight and wildness. Where water takes its first leap from the top, it is cool, and collected, and uninteresting, and mathematical, but it is when it finds that it has got into a scrape, and has farther to go than it thought for, that its character comes out; it is then that it begins to writhe, and twist, and sweep out zone after zone in wilder stretching as it falls, and to send down the rocket-like, lance-pointed, whizzing shafts at its sides, sounding for the bottom. And it is this prostration, this hopeless abandonment of its ponderous power to the air, which is always peculiarly expressed by Turner, and especially in the case before us; while our other artists, keeping to the parabolic line, where they do not lose themselves in smoke and foam, make their cataract look muscular and wiry, and may consider themselves fortunate if they can keep it from stopping. I believe the majesty of motion which Turner has given by these concentric catenary lines must be felt even by those who have never seen a high waterfall, and therefore cannot appreciate their exquisite fidelity to nature.

—*Modern Painters*, Vol. I, "Of Water, As Painted by Turner" (1843)

★

{"the noblest sea [. . .] certainly ever painted by man, is that of the *Slave Ship*"}

[. . .] the noblest sea that Turner has ever painted, and, if so, the noblest certainly ever painted by man, is that of the *Slave Ship*, the chief Academy picture of the Exhibition of 1840.[30] It is a sunset on the Atlantic after prolonged storm; but the storm is partially lulled, and the torn and streaming rain-clouds are moving in scarlet lines to lose themselves in the hollow of the night. The whole surface of sea included in the picture is divided into two ridges of enormous swell, not high, nor local, but a low, broad heaving of the whole ocean, like the lifting of its bosom by deep-drawn breath after the torture of the

[30] J. M. W. Turner, *The Slave Ship*, 1840, painting.

storm. Between these two ridges, the fire of the sunset falls along the trough of the sea, dyeing it with an awful but glorious light, the intense and lurid splendor which burns like gold and bathes like blood. Along this fiery path and valley, the tossing waves by which the swell of the sea is restlessly divided, lift themselves in dark, indefinite, fantastic forms, each casting a faint and ghastly shadow behind it along the illumined foam. They do not rise everywhere, but three or four together in wild groups, fitfully and furiously, as the under strength of the swell compels or permits them; leaving between them treacherous spaces of level and whirling water, now lighted with green and lamp-like fire, now flashing back the gold of the declining sun, now fearfully dyed from above with the indistinguishable images of the burning clouds, which fall upon them in flakes of crimson and scarlet, and give to the reckless waves the added motion of their own fiery flying. Purple and blue, the lurid shadows of the hollow breakers are cast upon the mist of the night, which gathers cold and low, advancing like the shadow of death upon the guilty ship as it labors amidst the lightning of the sea, its thin masts written upon the sky in lines of blood, girded with condemnation in that fearful hue which signs the sky with horror, and mixes its flaming flood with the sunlight,—and cast far along the desolate heave of the sepulchral waves, incarnadines the multitudinous sea.

I believe, if I were reduced to rest Turner's immortality upon any single work, I should choose this. Its daring conception—ideal in the highest sense of the word—is based on the purest truth, and wrought out with the concentrated knowledge of a life; its colour is absolutely perfect, not one false or morbid hue in any part or line, and so modulated that every square inch of canvas is a perfect composition; its drawing as accurate as fearless; the ship buoyant, bending, and full of motion; its tones as true as they are wonderful; and the whole picture dedicated to the most sublime of subjects and impressions—(completing thus the perfect system of all truth, which we have shown to be formed by Turner's works)—the power, majesty, and deathfulness of the open, deep, illimitable Sea.

—*Modern Painters*, Vol. I, "Of Water, As Painted by Turner" (1843)

★

{"it is on him [. . .] that all modern landscape has been founded"}

Turner was equally great in all the elements of landscape, and it is on him, and on his daring additions to the received schemes of landscape art, that all modern landscape has been founded. You will never meet any truly great living landscape painter who will not at once frankly confess his obligations to Turner, not, observe, as having copied him, but as having been led by Turner to look in nature for what he would otherwise either not have discerned, or discerning, not have dared to represent.

Turner, therefore, was the first man who presented us with the *type* of perfect landscape art: and the richness of that art, with which you are at present surrounded, and which enables you to open your walls as it were into so many windows, through which you can see whatever has charmed you in the fairest scenery of your country, you will do well to remember as *Turneresque*. [. . .]

But Turner's work is yet only begun. His greatness is, as yet, altogether denied by many; and to the full, felt by very few. But every day that he lies in his grave will bring some new acknowledgment of his power; and through those eyes, now filled with dust, generations yet unborn will learn to behold the light of nature.

—*Lectures on Architecture and Painting*, "Turner and His Works" (1853)

★

{"it is only the clumsy and uninventive artist who thinks"}

I say he "*thinks*" this, and "introduces" that. But, strictly speaking, he does not think at all. If he thought, he would instantly go wrong; it is only the clumsy and uninventive artist who thinks. All these changes come into his head involuntarily; an entirely imperative dream, crying, "Thus it must be," has taken possession of him; he can see and do, not otherwise than as the dream directs.

This is especially to be remembered with respect to the next incident—the introduction of figures. Most persons to whom I have shown the drawing (*Pass of Faido*), and who feel its general character, regret that there is any living thing in it; they say it destroys the majesty of its desolation. But the dream said not so to Turner. The dream insisted particularly upon the great fact of its having come by the road. The torrent was wild, the stones were wonderful; but the most wonderful thing of all was how we ourselves, the dream and I, ever got there. By our feet we could not—by the clouds we could not—by any ivory gates we could not—in no other wise could we have come than by the coach road. One of the great elements of sensation, all the day long, has been that extraordinary road, and its goings on, and gettings about; here, under avalanches of stones and among insanities of torrents, and overhangings of precipices, much tormented and driven to all manner of makeshifts and coils to this side and the other, still the marvelous road persists in going on, and that so smoothly and safely, that it is not merely great diligences, going in a caravanish manner, with whole teams of horses, that can traverse it, but little post-chaises with small postboys, and a pair of ponies. And the dream declared that the full essence and soul of the scene, and consummation of the wonderfulness of the torrents and Alps, lay in a post-chaise, with small ponies and postboy, which accordingly it insisted upon Turner's inserting, whether he liked it or not, at the turn of the road.

—*Modern Painters*, Vol. IV, "Of Turnerian Topography" (1856)

★

{"he seems never to have lost, or cared to disturb, the impression made upon him by any scene"}

[. . .] with all those whom I have carefully studied (Dante, Scott, Turner, and Tintoret) it seems to me to hold absolutely; their imagination consisting, not in a voluntary production of new images, but an involuntary remembrance, exactly at the right moment, of something they had actually seen.

Imagine all that any of these men had seen or heard in the whole course of their lives, laid up accurately in their memories as in vast storehouses, extending, with the poets, even to the slightest intonations of syllables heard in the beginning of their lives, and with the painters, down to the minute folds of drapery, and shapes of leaves or stones; and over all this unindexed and immeasurable mass of treasure, the imagination brooding and wandering, but dream-gifted, so as to summon at any moment exactly such groups of ideas as shall justly fit each other: this I conceive to be the real nature of the imaginative mind, and this, I believe, it would be oftener explained to us as being, by the men themselves who possess it, but that they have no idea what the state of other persons' minds is in comparison; they suppose every one remembers all that he has seen in the same way, and do not understand how it happens that they alone can produce good drawings or great thoughts.

Whether this be the case with all inventions or not, it was assuredly the case with Turner to such an extent that he seems never to have lost, or cared to disturb, the impression made upon him by any scene,—even in his earliest youth. He never seems to have gone back to a place to look at it again, but, as he gained power to have painted and repainted it as first seen, associating with it certain new thoughts or new knowledge, but never shaking the central pillar of the old image.

—*Modern Painters*, Vol. IV, "Of Turnerian Topography" (1856)

*

{"said Turner, '[. . .] but my business is to draw what I see, and not what I know is there'"}

[. . .] Turner, in his early life, was sometimes good-natured, and would show people what he was about. He was one day making a drawing of Plymouth harbour, with some ships at the distance of a mile or two, seen against the light. Having shown this drawing to a naval officer, the naval officer observed with surprise, and objected with very justifiable indignation, that the ships of the line had no port-holes. "No," said Turner, "certainly not. If you will walk up to Mount Edgecumbe, and look at the ships against the sunset, you will find you can't see the port-holes." "Well, but," said the naval officer, still indignant, "you know the port-holes are there." "Yes," said Turner, "I know that well enough; but my business is to draw what I see, and not what I know is there."

Now that is the law of all fine artistic work whatsoever; and, more than that, it is, on the whole, perilous to you, and undesirable, that you *should* know what is there. If, indeed, you have so perfectly disciplined your sight that it cannot be influenced by prejudice;—if you are sure that none of your knowledge of what is there will be allowed to assert itself; and that you can reflect the ship as simply as the sea beneath it does, though you may know it with the intelligence of a sailor,—then, indeed, you may allow yourself the pleasure, and what will sometimes be the safeguard from error, of learning what ships, or stars, or mountains, are in reality. But the ordinary powers of human perception are almost certain to be disturbed by the knowledge of the real nature of what they draw; and until you are quite fearless of your faithfulness to the appearances of things, the less you know of their reality the better.

—*The Eagle's Nest*, "The Relation to Art of the Sciences of Inorganic Form" (1872)

Works Cited

The works of Ruskin cited below are available online through Project Gutenberg, the Internet Archive, or HathiTrust.

Aesthetic and Mathematic Schools of Art in Florence: Lectures Given Before the University of Oxford in Michaelmas Term, 1874.

Arata Pentelici: Seven Lectures on the Elements of Sculpture, Given Before the University of Oxford in Michaelmas Term, 1870.

Art of England.

Eagle's Nest: Ten Lectures on the Relation of Natural Science to Art, Given Before the University of Oxford in Lent Term, 1872.

Fors Clavigera: Letters to the Workmen and Labourers of Great Britain.

"Inaugural Address Delivered at the Cambridge School of Art." (October 29, 1858.)

Laws of Fesole.

Lectures on Architecture and Painting, Delivered at Edinburgh in November 1853.

Lectures on Art, Delivered Before the University of Oxford in Hilary Term, 1870.

Modern Painters (five volumes).

Mornings in Florence.

Pre-Raphaelitism.

Quarterly Review (review of *The History of Christian Art* by Lord Lindsay, June 1847; "Eastlake on the History of Painting," March 1848).

Queen of the Air.

Seven Lamps of Architecture

Stones of Venice (three volumes).

Two Paths: Being Lectures on Art, and Its Application to Decoration and Manufacture, Delivered in 1858–9.

Selected Bibliography

Clark, Kenneth. *Ruskin Today*. Harmondsworth: Penguin. 1967.

Collingwood, W. G. *The Life of John Ruskin*. Houghton, Mifflin and Company. 1902.

Fagence-Cooper, Suzanne. *To See Clearly: Why Ruskin Matters*. Quercus Publishing. 2020.

Gayford, Martin. *Venice: City of Pictures*. Thames and Hudson. 2023.

Hilton, Tim. *John Ruskin: The Early Years*. Yale University Press. 1985.

Hilton, Tim. *John Ruskin: The Later Years*. Yale University Press. 2000.

Hunt, John Dixon. *The Wider Sea: A Life of John Ruskin*. Dent. 1982.

Rosenberg, John D. *The Genius of John Ruskin: Selections from His Writings*. University of Virginia Press. 1998.

Ruskin, John. *John Ruskin: On Genius*. Edited by Bob Blaisdell. Hesperus. 2011.

Ruskin, John. *On the Old Road: A Collection of Miscellaneous Essays and Articles on Art and Literature*. George Allen. 1899.

Ruskin, John. *Selected Prose of Ruskin*. Edited by Matthew Hodgart. Signet. 1972.

Ruskin, John. *The Lamp of Beauty: Writings on Art by John Ruskin*. Edited by Joan Evans. Cornell University Press. 1980.

Ruskin, John. *The Works of John Ruskin*. Edited by E. T. Cook and Alexander Wedderburn. London: George Allen. (See "The Complete Works of John Ruskin": lancaster.ac.uk/the-ruskin/the-complete-works-of-ruskin/.) 1903–1912.

Sdegno, Emma. *Looking at Tintoretto with John Ruskin: A Venetian Anthology*. Marsilio. 2018.